Setting Up a Company in the European Community

A Country by Country Guide

Setting Up a Company in the European Community

A Country by Country Guide

Compiled by

Brebner & Co

ORYX PRESS
1989

The information contained herein is not intended to be exhaustive, but to provide the reader with information which will enable him or her to achieve a general awareness and understanding of the topics dealt with.

We take no responsibility if clients rely on the information contained herein without obtaining confirmation in writing from us in relation to their specific requirements.

Brebner & Co.
International Division
November 1988

The rare Arabian Oryx is believed to have inspired the myth of the unicorn. This desert antelope became virtually extinct in the early 1960s. At that time several groups of international conservationists arranged to have 9 animals sent to the Phoenix Zoo to be the nucleus of a captive breeding herd. Today the Oryx population is nearly 800, and over 400 have been returned to reserves in the Middle East.

© Brebner & Co., International Division 1989

Published in the United States by
The Oryx Press
2214 North Central at Encanto
Phoenix, Arizona 85004-1483

Published in the United Kingdom by
Kogan Page
120 Pentonville Road
London N1 9JN
England

Published simultaneously in Canada

Printed in the United Kingdom

Library of Congress Cataloging-in-Publication Data
Setting up a company in the European Community.
    Includes index.
    1. Corporation law – European Economic Community
countries. I. Brebner and Co. International Division.

KJE2448.S47   1989   346.4′ 066   89-8691
ISBN 0-89774-601-5   344.0666

CONTENTS

FRANCE

GERMANY (FEDERAL REPUBLIC OF)

GREECE

IRELAND (REPUBLIC OF)

ITALY

LUXEMBOURG

THE NETHERLANDS

PORTUGAL

SPAIN

UNITED KINGDOM

FOREWORD

The London Chamber of Commerce and Industry is delighted to be endorsing this book which we feel will be of immense benefit to businesses hoping to take advantage of the unified common market of the European Communities.

We see it as our particular role to support the concepts of reducing the burdens on businesses which arise from a fragmented market in Europe. We continue to act in our representational capacity to promote a better business environment in Europe.

London is in a unique position and, as the leading Chamber of Commerce for this capital city and major access point into the European Community, we are well positioned to assist all businesses that wish to participate in this exciting and vastly increased market.

We strongly believe that businesspeople can only act effectively if they have a comprehensive knowledge of the different rules which apply in this area. The Chamber therefore provides sources of information, training and language facilities, and, indeed, publications to meet the educational needs of business. This book is part of that process.

Anthony Platt
Chief Executive
London Chamber of Commerce and Industry

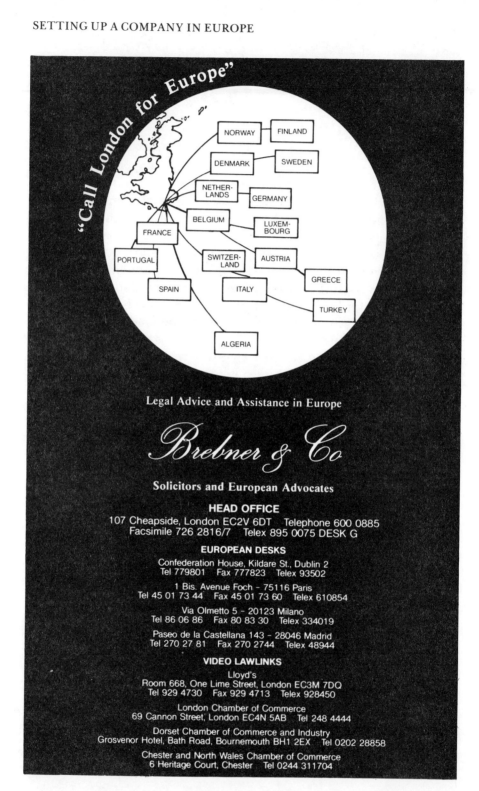

PREFACE

Probably the most significant aspect of the thrust towards 1992 will be the differences it highlights rather than the harmony it produces.

Effective moves towards the unification of laws and regulations throughout the EC will only come when enough people find the differences so inconvenient and unnecessary that total harmonisation becomes the only practical response of the various national governments. Bruxelles may help us to be European in the future but, in the meantime, it will be the tide of expanding business interests and the currents of individual imagination that will make us become European.

This guide is designed to familiarise business people with some standard company structures they may choose to use when developing operations beyond their own national boundaries. It will hopefully prove to be a useful and practical reference source for both them and their advisers.

There are, of course, other ways of setting up in another country: agencies, distributors, franchises, licences and so on, but as long as frontiers continue to exert their influences and as long as ambition drives enterprises to establish a physical presence in a foreign country, a subsidiary company will continue to enjoy pride of place.

I acknowledge the efforts of the legal staff in the firm's various country groups who helped collate the information. I know and they know where the greatest merits lie. A special thanks also to those at the London Chamber of Commerce for their inspiration and to Theo Sioufas and his firm in Athens without whom we could not have made a common market dozen!

John S Brebner
London, December 1988

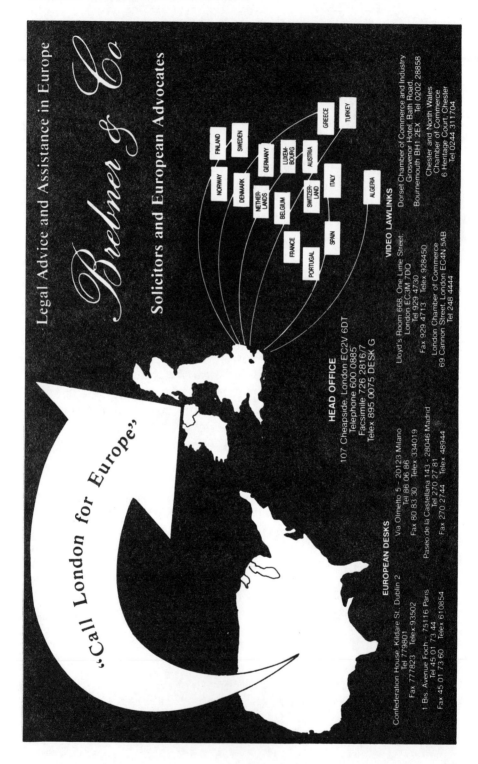

Legal Advice and Assistance in Europe

Bretner & Co

Solicitors and European Advocates

"Call London for Europe"

NORWAY
FINLAND
SWEDEN
DENMARK
GERMANY
NETHER-LANDS
LUXEM-BOURG
GREECE
TURKEY
BELGIUM
AUSTRIA
SWITZER-LAND
ITALY
ALGERIA
FRANCE
SPAIN
PORTUGAL

HEAD OFFICE
107 Cheapside, London EC2V 6DT
Telephone 600 0885
Facsimile 726 2816/7
Telex 895 0075 DESK G

EUROPEAN DESKS

Confederation House, Kildare St, Dublin 2
Tel 779801
Fax 777823 Telex 93502

1 Bis, Avenue Foch – 75116 Paris
Tel 45 01 73 44
Fax 45 01 73 60 Telex 610854

Via Olmetto 5 – 20123 Milano
Tel 86 06 86
Fax 80 83 30 Telex 334019

Paseo de la Castellana 143 - 28046 Madrid
Tel 270 27 81
Fax 270 2744 Telex 48944

VIDEO LAWLINKS

Lloyd's Room 668, One Lime Street,
London EC3M 7DQ
Tel 929 4730
Fax 929 4713 Telex 928450

London Chamber of Commerce
69 Cannon Street, London EC4N 5AB
Tel 248 4444

Dorset Chamber of Commerce and Industry
Grosvenor Hotel, Bath Road,
Bournemouth BH1 2EX Tel 0202 28858

Chester and North Wales
Chamber of Commerce
6 Heritage Court, Chester
Tel 0244 317704

INTRODUCTION

Each of the twelve Members of the European Community (EC) has its own legislation governing company formation and administration. Although there are certain general features common to them all, each national company law has its own unique requirements, reflecting different traditions and concerns. Other divergences may arise because two Members – the United Kingdom and the Republic of Ireland – are common law jurisdictions, while all the others have a civil law heritage.

This survey does not attempt to describe all the various structures which businessmen may adopt in each Member country to carry on their activities. Rather, attention focuses upon the two forms of company organisation which the foreign investor may find most useful in the countries surveyed. For ease of reference, these are referred to very generally as 'private' and 'public' companies although technically they may differ from country to country.

A description and summary of the essential provisions of the company formation laws of the various EC Member States would, however, be incomplete without reference to Community attempts to create and impose uniform standards upon the organisation and administration of cross-frontier business structures.

Since 1970 the various constitutive organs of the EC have intermittently discussed and considered the contents of a European Company Statute. As presently conceived, the statute would provide a completely new set of rules governing company formation and registration, capital requirements, shareholders rights, meetings and management structure and would eliminate those differences in taxation policy which discourage companies from cross-frontier cooperation.

To date, efforts to enact a common transnational European Company Statute have foundered largely on differences in attitudes within the EC on worker participation in company decision-making processes, uncertainty over the extent to which the Statute would take precedence over national law, disagreements over equity

15

participation limits on non-EC shareholders and concern over tax implications.

Pending approval of a uniform European Company Statute, the EC Council of Ministers in July 1985 adopted Regulation No 2137/85 which provides for a new type of vehicle for cross-frontier cooperation between firms established in different EC Member countries. Known as the European Economic Interest Grouping (EEIG), it combines some elements of several familiar business structures with a continuing joint venture concept. It is designed to be particularly useful to companies wishing to engage in, for example, joint research and development, purchasing, production and selling, quality control and consortia to bid for public and private contracts.

An EEIG is formed by contractual agreement between at least two members who may be natural persons working in or providing services within the EC, or juridical persons formed in accordance with the laws of an EC Member State.

The contract of formation must contain as a minimum the name of the Grouping, followed by the words 'European Economic Interest Grouping' or 'EEIG', the registered address, the objects, duration and basic information on each member of the Grouping. It must be registered in the State where the Grouping has its official address, along with any changes in the members, amendments to the contract, appointment of managers and notices of liquidation or closure.

The Regulation does not establish any capital requirements. Members are free to decide in the contract the amount and form of their investment in the Grouping. No contributions may be solicited from the public. Although the EEIG is a legal person, capable of entering into contracts and of suing and being sued, its members do not have limited liability.

The EEIG is managed through two bodies, the members acting collectively (akin to a shareholders' meeting) and a manager or managers (akin to a board of directors), designated in the contract or by the members. At meetings each member normally has one vote. The contract, however, may allow more than one vote for certain members, provided no single member has a majority.

The contract may prescribe the conditions for a quorum and the majorities needed for decisions. However, certain actions must be approved unanimously. These include changes in the objects and voting requirements, extension of the Grouping's duration and changes in the members or to their contributions to the grouping's financing.

Although the Regulation establishes a limited type of supranational law to govern the EEIG, national and other community laws on social security, competition and protection of intellectual property will still apply. Profits are to be apportioned to the members according to the contract and are taxable under their respective national laws.

The EEIG Regulation will not come into effect until 1 July 1989, in order to give Member States time in which to make their legislation compatible with its requirements and to establish procedures for registration laws. The development of the EEIG may therefore be viewed as a possible transitional phase pending the acceptance of a more specific, comprehensive European Statute.

The Community has to date been more successful in imposing company law uniformity through the use of Directives, which seek to harmonise basic provisions in national company legislation to safeguard the interests of shareholders and creditors.

The following Directives should by now have been incorporated into national legislation:

The First Directive (68/151 of 9 March 1968) concerns the maintenance of the registries, filing accounts and other documents and their availability to the public, as well as rules to protect third parties against a company's lack of legal capacity or that of its organs.
The Second Directive (77/91 of 13 December 1976) applies to public limited companies and fixes a minimum required capital of 25,000 Ecu to be subscribed before a company may be incorporated or obtain authorisation to commence business.
The Third Directive (78/855 of 9 October 1978) coordinates national laws on mergers of public limited companies within one Member State as far as the protection of rights of shareholders and third parties is concerned.
The Fourth Directive (78/660 of 25 July 1978) relates to the annual accounts of public and private limited companies and, in particular, to the presentation and contents of annual accounts and annual reports, the valuation methods used therein and their publication.
The Sixth Directive 82/891 of 17 December 1982) complements the Third Directive on mergers and relates to the division, within one Member State, of public limited companies.

The Seventh Directive (83/349 of 13 June 1983) coordinates national legislations governing consolidated accounts. (It does not apply to banks and insurance companies.)

The Eight Directive (84/253 of 10 April 1984) lays down minimum standards for the qualifications of auditors.

Other Directives are still being negotiated in the Council.

The Fifth Directive concerns the structure of the boards of public limited companies, the powers and obligations of executive and non-executive directors and employee participation in the management.

The Ninth Directive relates to the structure of groups of companies containing a public limited company as a subsidiary.

The Tenth Directive covers mergers between public limited companies registered in different Member States.

The Eleventh Directive relates to the accounts of branches of companies established in another Member State or in a third country.

The Twelfth Directive would enable individuals to form themselves into limited companies.

Seeking harmonisation through Directives is admittedly cumbersome and piecemeal and therefore efforts to reach agreement on a single, general legal framework will continue in order to provide businessmen with an additional and optional legal framework for cross-border industrial cooperation.

Despite the lack of agreement to date, it seems likely that a uniform company law statute eventually will be enacted and, consequently, developments should be closely monitored. No matter what the outcome, however, national laws will for the foreseeable future co-exist with any such supranational legislation.

LONDON
CHAMBER *of* COMMERCE

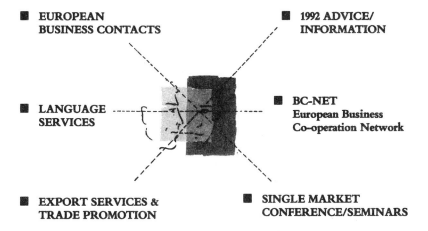

■ **EUROPEAN**
BUSINESS CONTACTS

■ **1992 ADVICE/**
INFORMATION

■ **LANGUAGE**
SERVICES

■ **BC-NET**
European Business
Co-operation Network

■ **EXPORT SERVICES &**
TRADE PROMOTION

■ **SINGLE MARKET**
CONFERENCE/SEMINARS

The London Chamber of Commerce is the largest privately funded organisation of its kind in the world. With over 100 years of committed support to international and domestic trade development, the Chamber continues to provide its members with the contacts, services and representation that enables business to prosper.

Membership gives your company access to expert staff providing one of the widest range of business services available 'under one roof' today.

IN BUSINESS TO HELP BUSINESS

IF YOU WOULD LIKE TO KNOW MORE, CONTACT:
ROGER FISHER, HEAD OF MARKETING AND MEMBERSHIP,
LONDON CHAMBER OF COMMERCE, 69 CANNON STREET,
LONDON EC4N 5AB.
TEL: 01-248 4444,   TELEX: 888941 LCCI G   FAX: 01-489 0391

19

BELGIUM

PRIVATE COMPANY
(Société Privée à Responsabilité Limitée/Besloten Vennootschap
met Beperkte Aansprakelijkheid)

PUBLIC COMPANY
(Société Anonyme/Naamloze Vennootschap)

INTRODUCTION

This section examines two types of company. The first is the *Société Privée à Responsabilité Limitée/Besloten Vennootschap met Beperkte Aansprakelijkheid* (SPRL/BVBA), referred to as a private company. The second type is the *Société Anonyme/Naamloze Vennootschap* (SA/ NV), referred to as a public company. Both are limited companies.

The minimum legal capital for the SPRL/BVBA is BF 750,000 and for the SA/NV BF 1,250,000.

Both types of company are governed by the same fundamental legal texts, the major differences being the size of the capital and the nature of the shares.

Only shares in an SA/NV can be listed on the stock exchange.

No permit or prior authorisation is required for the formation of a company. However, a number of closely defined activities or trades, often connected with specific products, are subject to certain regulations and may be subject to prior authorisation.

Foreign capital may be brought into Belgium without restriction, in whatever currency, provided that the transfer is channelled through the financial market. No prior authorisation from the Exchange Control Authority is required.

PRIVATE COMPANY

(Société Privée à Responsabilité Limitée/Besloten Vennootschap met Beperkte Aansprakelijkheid)

Documents

Memorandum and Articles of Association: (les statuts/statuten)
The document must contain the following information:

- type and official name of the company;
- exact indication of the aims and objectives;
- exact address of the registered offices;
- identity of the promoters;
- duration of the company if it is not unlimited;
- total amount of underwritten share capital and the amount of capital that has been issued;
- number and nominal value of the shares and conditions for future transfer;
- financial institution with which the disposable capital investments have been deposited;
- dealings for value to which the real property assets have been subjected during the previous five years;
- mortgages and liens attached to company assets;
- conditions for the exercise of optional rights;
- details of each investment in kind:
    - name of the investor,
    - name of the auditor,
    - conclusion of his report,
    - nominal value of shares issued against each investment;
- number and title of the persons responsible for the representation of the company as regards third parties, day to day management, supervision, control of the company and distribution of functions;
- beginning and end of the business year;
- date and time of the general meeting of shareholders;
- nature of the benefits offered to each of the founders;
- the approximate cost of incorporation.

The SPRL/BVBA must be formed in the presence of a notary. The founders appear in person or by proxy before the notary who records the memorandum in an original deed.

Minute Book
A minute book of the board's meetings and a minute book of the shareholders' meetings must be kept by the SPRL/BVBA.

Accounting Books
An SPRL/BVBA must keep books of account and certain records in accordance with accounting, tax and social security regulations.

All Belgian companies or Belgian branch offices of foreign companies must file annual accounts with the Commercial Court Office (*Greffe du Tribunal de Commerce/Griffie van de Handelsrechtbank*) of the area where they are established. Local Commercial Court offices subsequently send copies of those annual accounts to the Central Registry Office (*Centrale des Bilans/Balanscentrale*) where they are available for public inspection.

Registration Requirements

Commercial Court
Within 15 days after the statutes are drawn up, extracts of the statutes must be deposited at the Commercial Court for publication in the Appendix to the Official Gazette. They have to be published in the official language (that is in either Flemish or French) of that section of the country where the company is to be located.

Registration with the trade register is required and the name of the Commercial Court of registration as well as the registration number must appear on all deeds, notices, publications, letterheads, invoices, purchase orders and other documents issued by the company.

Bank Account
Every commercial company is obliged to open a bank account with a Belgian financial institution.

The bank account number must appear on every invoice or statement requesting payment.

VAT Office
All persons and corporations whose activity includes the delivery of goods or the supply of services mentioned in the VAT Code are to

be registered with the VAT administration as VAT taxable persons and the application form request for a VAT number must be filed with the local VAT office.

National Office for Social Security
Any company operating in Belgium and employing one or more workers, whether incorporated in Belgium or elsewhere, comes under the national security system and has therefore to register with the National Office for Social Security.

Capital Requirements

Minimum Amount
The minimum capital is BF 750,000. The whole capital must be fully subscribed, must at least amount to BF 750,000, with a minimum of BF 250,000 paid in.

Each share must be paid up to the extent of at least 20 per cent, subject to the condition that the total amount of paid up shares be no less than BF 250,000.

Type of Capital Paid In
Subscriptions can be made in cash or in kind. In the case of contributions which are not in cash, a company auditor must be appointed by the founders before the company can be incorporated.

The auditor reports on the description of each contribution in kind and on the methods of evaluation used, and indicates the value allotted in exchange for these contributions.

Limits to Liability
Each shareholder's liability is limited to his contribution to the capital.

Ownership

Type of Ownership
Ownership is represented by *parts sociales* (for convenience hereafter referred to as shares).

The capital is divided into shares of a minimum nominal value of BF 1,000. The value must be identical for all shares.

Beneficiary shares cannot be issued. The shares must be issued to a named party and have to be entered in the shareholders register.

For this type of company there must be at least two shareholders (*associés/vennoten*). Before the law of 15 July 1985 only individuals could be shareholders in the SPRL/BVBA. Corporations could not be shareholders and thus the SPRL/BVBA was not commonly used by foreign investors. It is now possible for a legal entity to be shareholder in an SPRL/BVBA so that this type of company now qualifies as a vehicle for foreign subsidiary-type operations in Belgium.

Voting Rights

All shareholders have a number of votes directly proportional to the number of shares they possess. Each share gives the right to one vote but restrictions are imposed on voting power to protect minority interests.

Shareholders may vote in writing or by proxy.

Resolutions at the shareholders meeting are adopted by a simple majority of the votes present or represented at the meeting. For certain matters special quorums and majorities are required (amendments to the memorandum and articles of association, modifications of the purpose clause, increase or decrease of capital, early dissolution of the company).

Protection of Minority Owners

A general meeting of shareholders may be called at the request of shareholders representing at least 20 per cent of the share capital, but the voting power of shareholders is limited to protect minority interests. No shareholder, irrespective of the proportion of capital he holds, may cast a vote in excess of what would amount to a holding of one-fifth of the capital. An additional limitation is that he may not cast votes exceeding two-fifths of the total number of votes present or represented at the general meeting, whatever their proportion of the total.

Transfer of Ownership

Conditions for transfer of shares to outside parties are prescribed by law. The consent of at least half of the shareholders, representing at least three-quarters of the capital, is required.

The company statutes may provide further restrictions on the transfer of shares.

Dissolution/Winding Up

A special shareholders' meeting may decide at any time to dissolve the company. The decision must be taken at a meeting representing at least half of the corporate capital and by an affirmative vote of three-quarters of the shares voting.

If the company has lost half its capital, the directors must submit to the shareholders the question of whether to continue the corporate activities or to dissolve the company. The decision to dissolve requires the affirmative vote of at least three-quarters of the shares voting.

If the capital is reduced below BF 250,000, any person with a legitimate interest can ask the Commercial Court for dissolution of the company.

Following the decision to dissolve the company, the company will be deemed to exist for liquidation purposes only.

The liquidation is carried out by one or more liquidators who are appointed by the shareholders meeting deciding to dissolve the company.

Management

Board of Directors
An SPRL/BVBA is managed by one or more managing directors (*gérants/zaakvoerders*), who must be individuals but do not have to be shareholders of the SPRL/BVBA. There is no residence or nationality requirement on the managing directors and they may be appointed in the Articles or elected by the shareholders for a limited or indefinite period. The statutes determine the deliberation procedures for their election but in the absence of specific provisions, the managing directors are elected by simple majority of the shareholders.

Their power can only be withdrawn in full or in part for serious cause.

They exercise all the corporate powers of management and disposition within the framework of the company's objects.

The company is bound by the acts done by the managing directors even if those acts are not within the objects of the company (unless it can be proved that the third party knew that the act was outside the objects, for which purpose disclosure of the statutes is not of itself sufficient proof).

The managing directors must prepare an annual inventory, annual accounts (balance sheet and profit and loss accounts) and a management report all of which must be submitted to the general meeting of shareholders.

Employee Representation

Companies with 100 employees or more must set up a works council (*conseil d'entreprise/ondernemingsraad*) composed of an equal number of employer and employee representatives.

The works council must be convened at least once a month and its function is to review the employment policies and practices of the company, establish work rules and codetermine the work organisation, working conditions and overall activities of the enterprise.

Statutory Auditors

All SPRL/BVBAs over a certain size have to be audited by one or more statutory auditors who have to be members of the Belgian Institute of Company Auditors.

The size criteria are as follows:

- annual turnover of BF 145,000,000;
- balance sheet totals BF 70,000,000;
- annual average of 50 persons employed.

As from 1 March 1986 the law requires that all companies meeting these criteria appoint a statutory auditor at the first annual general meeting.

As from 28 February 1987 branches of foreign companies and other forms of business entity with over 100 employees must appoint an auditor.

The general meeting of shareholders appoints the statutory auditor usually upon a proposal of the board.

The statutes or the general meeting decide on the number of auditors required. Where more than one statutory auditor is appointed, they form a 'college'.

The statutory auditor must audit the financial situation of the company, the annual accounts and the propriety of the transactions underlying the annual accounts and give his opinion of these matters in a report addressed to the shareholders 15 days before the annual general meeting.

Formation Expenses and Taxation

Costs of Registering and Forming a Company

The expenditure involved (which is tax deductible) includes the following:

- registration tax of one per cent of the subscribed capital;

- notarial fees, calculated as a proportion of the total share capital;
- registration of proxies, copies etc (BF 10,000);
- cost of publication in the Belgian Official Gazette (BF 2,500 per typed page);
- registration with the Register of Commerce (BF 2,000).

Corporate Income Tax

The company income tax rate is fixed at 43 per cent on taxable income in excess of BF 16,600,000. Income below this amount is taxed at rates ranging from 30 per cent to 43 per cent, unless the company is a holding company or is at least 50 per cent owned by another company, in which case the 43 per cent rate applies at all levels.

Taxable income is based on the income as reported in the annual financial statements and includes all profits and losses, including speculative and non-speculative gains and losses, dividends interests, royalties and rents. Most expenses incurred to produce and preserve income are tax deductible.

Income and withholding taxes of foreign countries are deductible if they cannot be credited against the Belgian tax under a double taxation agreement.

Capital gains realised on assets owned in Belgium for more than five years are normally taxed at 21.5 per cent. Such gains are tax-exempt provided the sales proceeds are re-invested within a period of three years. Other capital gains are taxed as ordinary income.

Fundamental Legislative Texts

- Civil Code Articles 1832 – 1873;
- Commercial Code, Book I, Titel IX (*Lois Coordonnées sur les sociétés commerciales/Gecoordoneerde Wetten op de handelsvennootschappen*);
- *Loi du 3 juillet 1956, modifiée par celle du 16 août 1963* (concerning registration at Commercial Courts);
- *Loi du 27 juin 1969* (concerning registration with Social Security Authorities);
- *Loi du 20 septembre 1948 and Arrêté Royal (AR) du 27 novembre 1973* (concerning works councils);
- *Loi du 17 juillet 1975* amended by *Loi du 1 juillet 1983* (concerning accounting requirements).

PUBLIC COMPANY

(Société Anonyme/
Naamloze Vennootschap)

Documents

Memorandum and Articles of Association (les statuts/statuten)
This document must contain the following information:

- type and official name of the company;
- exact indication of the aims and objectives;
- exact address of the registered offices;
- duration of the company if it is not unlimited;
- total amount of underwritten share capital and the amount of this capital that has been issued;
- amount of authorised share capital;
- number and title of the persons responsible for:
    - representation of the company with third parties,
    - day to day management,
    - supervision,
    - control of the company and distribution of functions within its various departments;
- number and nominal value of the shares (or number of shares without nominal value) and conditions for future transfer. The same information must be provided if there are several categories of shares, as well as the rights attached to each type of share;
- the number of shares held by non-directors and the rights and conditions attached thereto, including any transfer restrictions;
- named or bearer shares as well as the arrangements for their conversion;
- details of each investment in kind as well as the name of the investor, the name of the auditor and the conclusions of his report, the nominal value of shares issued against each investment;
- the identity of the persons who signed the memorandum of incorporation;
- the nature of the benefits offered to each of the founders;

- the approximate cost of incorporation;
- the financial institution with which the disposable capital investments have been deposited;
- assigns against payment to which the real property has been subjected during the last five years;
- mortgages and liens attached to company assets;
- the conditions attached to the exercise of options.

The SA/NV must be formed before a notary. The founders appear in person or by proxy before the notary who records the memorandum in an original deed.

Minute Book
An SA/NV must keep a minute book of board meetings and a minute book of shareholders' meetings.

Accounting Books
An SA/NV must keep books of account and certain records in accordance with accounting, tax and social security regulations.

All Belgian companies or Belgian branch offices of foreign companies must file annual accounts with the Commercial Court office (*Greffe du Tribunal de Commerce/Griffie van de Handelsrechtbank*) of the area where they are established.

Local Commercial Court offices subsequently send copies of those annual accounts to the Central Registry Office (*Centrale des Bilans/Balanscentrale*) where they are at the disposal of the public.

Registration Requirements

Commercial Court
Within 15 days after the statutes are drawn up, extracts of the statutes must be deposited at the Commercial Court for publication in the Appendix to the Official Gazette. They have to be published in the official language (Flemish or French) of that section of the country where the company is to be located.

Registration with the trade register is required and the name of the Commercial Court of registration as well as the registration number must appear on all deeds, notices, publications, letterheads, invoices, purchase orders and other documents issued by the company.

Bank Account
Every trading company is obliged to open a bank account with a Belgian financial institution in Belgium, and the bank account

number must appear on every invoice or statement requesting payment.

VAT Office

All persons and corporations whose activity includes the delivery of goods or the supply of services mentioned in the VAT Code are to be registered with the VAT adminsistration as VAT taxable persons and the application form request for a VAT number must be filed with the local VAT office.

National Office for Social Security

Any company operating in Belgium and employing one or more workers, whether it be incorporated in Belgium or elsewhere, comes under the national social security system and has therefore to register with the National Office for Social Security.

Capital Requirements

Minimum Amount

The minimum capital is BF 1,250,000.

The capital must be completely subscribed and at least one quarter of all contributions in cash or in kind must be effectively paid up.

Each share corresponding to a contribution shall be issued for at least 25 per cent of par. As soon as the company is incorporated, the share capital must be fully issued to a minimum amount of BF 1,250,000.

Type of Capital Paid In

Subscriptions can be made in cash or in kind. In the case of contributions which are not in cash, a company auditor must be appointed by the founders before the company can be incorporated. He reports on the description of each contribution in kind and on the methods of evaluation used and indicates the value allotted in exchange for these contributions.

Limits to Liability

Shareholders are only liable to the extent of their contribution to the capital.

Ownership

Type of Ownership
The participants in an SA/NV are shareholders.

There must be at least two founders (*associés/vennoten*).

The shareholders may be individuals or companies, residents or non-residents.

The shares may be in the form of bearer shares or issued to a named party.

Bearer shares may only be allocated if they have been issued in full. They may be with or without a par value.

The company may issue shares that do not represent share capital (*parts de fondateur/stichtersaandelen* or *parts bénéficiaires/winstaandelen*). These shares generally participate in profit distributions but do not carry voting rights unless the articles specifically grant them.

Voting Rights
All shares representing capital carry the right to vote. Shares that do not represent capital may also carry a right to vote if the corporate charter so provides and within the limits fixed by law.

Resolutions are adopted by a simple majority of the votes present or represented at the meeting.

Each share is considered to represent one vote.

For certain matters special quorums and majorities are required (amendments to the memorandum and articles of association, modification of the purpose clause, increase or decrease of capital, extension of the life of the corporation, early dissolution or merger, early dissolution when half of the capital has been lost, early dissolution when three-quarters of the capital has been lost).

Protection of Minority Owners
A general meeting of shareholders may be called at the request of shareholders representing at least 20 per cent of the share capital.

The voting powers of shareholders is limited to protect minority interests, so that no shareholder, irrespective of the proportion of capital he holds, may cast a vote in excess of what would appertain to a holding of one-fifth of the capital. An additional limitation is that he may not cast votes exceeding two-fifths of the total number of votes present or represented at the general meeting whatever be their proportion of the total.

Transfer of Ownership

The transfer of bearer shares is effected by the mere handing over of the share certificates. The transfer of registered shares is effected via an entry in the roll of registered shares. The use of registered shares permits the control of share transfers.

A complete prohibition of the transfer of shares is illegal and any restrictions on share transfers are closely scrutinised by the courts. The statutes often provide that the transfer of registered shares will be valid only if approved by the board of directors, but the board may not unreasonably block the transfer of shares.

Dissolution/Winding Up

A special shareholders' meeting may decide at any time to dissolve the company. The decision must be taken at a meeting representing at least half of the corporate capital and by an affirmative vote of three-quarters of the shares voting.

If the company has lost half of its capital, the directors must submit to the shareholders the question of whether to continue the corporate activities or to dissolve the company. The decision to dissolve requires the affirmative vote of at least three-quarters of the shares voting.

Following the decision to dissolve the company, the company will be deemed to exist for liquidation purposes only.

The liquidation is carried out by one or more liquidators who are appointed by the shareholders' meeting deciding to dissolve the company.

Management

Board of Directors

The SA/NV is managed by a board of at least three directors, appointed by the general meeting.

The directors may not be appointed for a period longer than six years but they may be re-elected. They do not have to be shareholders and there is no residence or nationality requirement. They form a deliberative board that adopts its resolutions in accordance with the quorums and majorities stipulated in the memorandum.

The board has the power to do everything necessary to achieve the purposes of the company except for matters for which the shareholders' consent is required by law.

Daily Management

The daily management of the company may be delegated by the board to one or more directors or to one or more persons who are not on the board, such as managers, supervisors or other agents.

Limitations on the daily management powers imposed by the board of directors have an internal effect only and cannot be invoked against third parties.

Employee Representation

Companies with 100 employees or more must set up a works council (*conseil d'entreprise/ondernemingsraad*) composed of an equal number of employer and employee representatives. It is seen as a body of deliberation and cooperation between management and employees.

The works council must be convened at least once a month and its function is to review the employment policies and practices of the company, establish work rules and codetermine the work organisation, working conditions and overall activities of the enterprise.

Statutory Auditors

All SPRL/BVBAs over a certain size have to be audited by one or more statutory auditors who have to be members of the Belgian Institute of Company Auditors.

The size criteria are as follows:

- annual turnover of BF 145,000,000;
- balance sheet totals BF 70,000,000;
- annual average of 50 persons employed.

As from 1 March 1986 the law requires that all companies meeting these criteria appoint a statutory auditor at the first annual general meeting.

As from 28 February 1987 branches of foreign companies and other forms of business entity with over 100 employees must appoint an auditor.

The general meeting of shareholders appoints the statutory auditor usually upon a proposal of the board.

The statutes or the general meeting decide on the number of auditors required. Where more than one statutory auditor is appointed, they form a 'college'.

The statutory auditor must audit the financial situation of the company, the annual accounts and the propriety of the transactions underlying the annual accounts and give his opinion of these matters in a report addressed to the shareholders 15 days before the annual general meeting.

Formation Expenses and Taxation

Costs of Registering and Forming a Company
The expenditure involved, which is tax deductible, includes the following:

- registration tax of one per cent of the subscribed capital;
- notarial fees, calculated as a proportion of the total share capital;
- registration of proxies, copies etc (BF 10,000);
- cost of publication in the Belgian Official Gazette (BF 2,500 per typed page);
- registration with the Register of Commerce (BF 2,000).

Corporate Income Tax
The company income tax rate is fixed at 43 per cent on taxable income in excess of BF 16,600,000. Income below this amount is taxed at rates ranging from 30 per cent to 43 per cent, unless the company is a holding company or is for at least 50 per cent owned by another company, in which case the 43 per cent rate applies at all levels.

Taxable income is based on the income as reported in the annual financial statements and includes all profits and losses, including speculative and non-speculative gains and losses, dividends interests, royalties and rents. Most expenses incurred to produce and preserve income are tax deductible.

Income and witholding taxes of foreign countries are deductible if they cannot be credited against the Belgian tax under a double taxation agreement.

Capital gains realised on assets owned in Belgium for more than five years are normally taxed at 21.5 per cent. Such gains are tax-exempt provided the sales proceeds are reinvested within a period of three years. Other capital gains are taxed as ordinary income.

Fundamental Legislative Texts

- Civil Code Articles 1832 – 1873;
- Commercial Code, Book I, Titel IX (*Lois Coordonnées sur les sociétés commerciales/Gecoordoneerde Wetten op de handelsvennootschappen*);
- *Loi du 3 juillet 1956, modifiée par celle du 16 août 1963* (concerning registration at Commercial Courts);

- *Loi du 27 juin 1969* (concerning registration with Social Security Authorities);
- *Loi du 20 septembre 1948 and AR du 27 novembre 1973* (concerning works councils);
- *Loi du 17 juillet 1975* amended by *Loi du 1 juillet 1983* (concerning accounting requirements).

DENMARK

PRIVATE COMPANY
(Anpartsselskaber)

PUBLIC COMPANY
(Aktieselskaber)

INTRODUCTION

This section examines two types of company. The first type is the *Anpartsselskab* (ApS), referred to as a private company. The second type is the *Aktieselskab* (A/S), referred to as a public company. Both are limited liability companies.

In the ApS the participants are not shareholders as such since no share certificates are issued. For convenience, however, the participants will be referred to as shareholders.

The minimum legal capital for the ApS is DKr 80,000 and for the A/S DKr 300,000.

Only shares in an A/S can be listed on the stock exchange.

In an A/S a share must carry a vote as opposed to the rules for an ApS where the shares need not carry a vote.

In an A/S the Internal Rules (*Vedtægter*) can be drafted so as to give shares for the same amount different voting power (a share cannot be given more than ten times the voting power compared to any other share for the same amount).

Operations in foreign currency may be effected only through banks and brokers authorised to deal in foreign exchange.

A non resident may make direct investments in Denmark without the permission of the Danish National Bank (*Nationalbanken*) provided the direct investment in each business entity does not exceed DKr 2m per calendar year. Permissions will where needed usually be granted.

A direct investment can be described as a permanent (at least five years) and material (at least 10 per cent of the equity in the enterprise) economic relationship with a Danish enterprise.

Even though the transaction may not require permission, all remittances to and from a foreign country exceeding DKr 10,000 must be reported to the Danish National Bank.

Foreign currency restrictions are not as such imposed on the repatriation of capital invested in a limited liability company.

The Danish VAT rate is fixed at 22 per cent.

PRIVATE COMPANY

(Anpartsselskaber)

Documents

Memorandum and Articles of Association (Stiftelsesdokument)
Stiftelsesdokumentet is one document in two parts constituting both the memorandum and articles of association. To avoid confusion the two parts of the document are referred to as Internal Rules (*Vedtægter*) and General Information. The memorandum and articles of association as a whole will be referred to as *Stiftelsesdokumentet*.

Internal Rules
The contents must specify:

- the name of the company and, if applicable, any additional names;
- the county where the head office of the company is to be located;
- the purpose of the company;
- the amount of capital to be paid in to the company, with a minimum of DKr 80,000;
- whether the subscribed capital is divided into several shares and if so, the nominal amount of the shares and the voting rights appertaining thereto;
- whether the company is to have a board and if so, the term of office and the number of board members (or the minimum and maximum number of board members);
- the term of office and the number of auditors;
- the procedure for calling a general meeting;
- what issues may be taken up by general meetings; and
- the fiscal year (which must be twelve months except for the first period, where it may be either shorter or longer but it cannot exceed eighteen months).

Where applicable the following must also be specified:

- an obligation on the shareholders to let the company or others take over their shares in part or wholly;

- any limitations as to the transfer of shares;
- special rights for certain shares;
- limitations in the subscription rights for board members and directors.

General Information

The contents must include:

- the names and addresses of the company's promoter(s), executive officers and auditors and, if any, the members of the board for the period until the first general meeting following the formation of the company;
- how the shares are divided among the promoters;
- the subscription price for the shares;
- the time limits for payment for the shares; and
- whether the preliminary expenses are to be paid by the company and if so, the maximum amount must be stated (this must not exceed 5 per cent of the capital).

The following information must also be provided together with a statement from the statutory auditor as to its accuracy:

- whether payment in kind may be made and if so, the valuation thereof (the payment in kind must be some kind of property and it must have an economic value but it cannot consist of a duty to provide services or work);
- whether the company is to take over such payment in exchange for shares;
- whether promoters or others will be given special rights or benefits; and
- whether special agreements, which will financially burden the company, are to be made with promoters or others.

If the company in formation is taking over an existing company an opening balance must be made by the statutory auditor and this must be enclosed.

Stiftelsesdokumentet must be signed by the promoters.

The promoters may in writing authorise another named person to act on their behalf. This authorisation must accompany the documents and the application form to be registered. Authorisation documents made in other countries must be either issued by the Danish Consul or an official notary.

The board must keep a list of all the shareholders containing names, addresses and the number of shares held.

Entries on the list must be dated.

Minute Book (Forhandlingsprotokollen)
Summaries of general meetings are kept in the minute book which is signed by the presiding chairman. The minute book or a copy thereof must be available for the shareholders for inspection at the company's office no longer than 14 days after the general meeting.

Accounting Books (Årsregnskab)
The annual accounts must consist of the following:

- a balance sheet (*Balance/Status*);
- a profit and loss statement (*Resultatøpgorelse*);
- notes (*Noter*);
- an annual report (*Årsberetning*);
- for parent companies the consolidated accounts of subsidiaries are also required.

Registration Form (Registreringsanmeldelsesblanket)
The forms for registration can be obtained from the local police station.

The information to be submitted must at least mention:

- the name and address of the company and also a postal address if different;
- the company's first financial year;
- the amount of capital raised, the amount paid in, the form of payment, the nominal amount of shares not fully paid, and when the remainder must be paid;
- the full names, titles and addresses of the promoter(s), board members, executive officers, auditors and of any substitutes.

The form must be accompanied by:

- *Stiftelsesdokumentet* and other documents relating to formation (either the originals or copies certified by the board). Documents relating to formation include conveyance deeds, leasing contracts, licensing contracts and any other relevant documents of this kind;
- evidence that at least one of the promoters is either resident in Denmark or is resident in another EC Member State;
- evidence that board members, executive officers and auditors are 18 years old or over and in good standing. It must be shown that all executive officers and at least half of the board

43

members are Danish residents or EC residents and that one or more of the auditors is a Danish resident and either *Stats-autoriseret Revisor* or *Registreret Revisor*.

- evidence that at least half the registered capital — and at least DKr 80,000 — has been paid in.

The application form must be signed by all board members (or by all executive officers if there is no board). The signatures must be certified by a notary, an *Advokat* or by two witnesses.

The documents must be in Danish.

Registration Requirements

Trade and Industry

Application must be made on a form obtainable from the local police station. The completed form with documents must be sent to the Companies Register (*Erhverus- og Selskabsstyrelsen*) at the following address:

Erhverus- og Selskabsstyrelsen
Kampmannsgade 1
1604 Copenhagen V.

The board must apply for registration within two months of the date of signing *Stiftelsesdokumentet*. Registration will be refused if the two months are exceeded.

The company is given a number when registered.

All registrations are immediately made public in *Statstidende*. Information made public in *Statstidende* is deemed to be known by third parties, with certain exceptions.

Tax Authority

Companies with employees must register with the local Inland Revenue (*Skattemyndighederne*) at the register called *Arbejds-giverregisteret*. Forms are obtainable from the local Inland Revenue Office.

VAT Authority

Companies must register with the Customs Officer (*Toldvæsenet*) to be placed on the VAT Register (*Momsregisteret*). Forms can be obtained from the local Customs Office.

Capital Requirements

Minimum Amount
The minimum authorised, issued and paid up capital is DKr 80,000.

The capital must have been fully subscribed and at least half of the capital, this not being less than DKr 80,000 in addition to any amounts paid for the shares in excess of the face value, must be paid in.

The remainder must be paid within a year after registration of the company.

The amount payable for a share must not be lower than the nominal amount of the share.

Type of Capital Paid In
Payment of the capital must actually be made. Payment is made when the control over the money or assets constituting the payment has moved from the shareholder to the company.

Payment can be made in kind but it must be property with an economic value. It cannot consist of a duty to provide services or work.

Limits to Liability
The shareholders are not personally liable for the obligations of the company. Joint liability will, however, be imposed for obligations entered into before registration of the company.

Registration of the the company results in a transfer of obligations to the company. The obligations in question must either have been mentioned in *Stiftelsesdokumentet* or have been incurred after the signing of *Stiftelsesdokumentet.*

Liability will be imposed on shareholders for intentional or negligent acts. The damages can be reduced under circumstances where it appears to be just to do so. If several persons are liable they will be liable jointly and severally.

Ownership

Type of Ownership
The participants in an *Anpartsselskab* are in fact participants (*Anpartshavere*) rather than shareholders, thus no share certificate is issued. For convenience the participants will be referred to as shareholders.

A receipt can be obtained certifying that the person is on the list of shareholders.

There is no duty upon the shareholders to appear on the list of shareholders but in relation to situations where notification is needed (eg when calling a general meeting) inclusion on the list is necessary.

For this type of company only one promoter is needed.

Voting Rights

All shares give equal rights in the company in relation to the nominal amount of the share, unless otherwise stated in *Stiftelsesdokumentet* under Internal Rules.

The shareholder can authorise a proxy to attend the general meeting on his behalf. Only the shareholder is entitled to bring an adviser, a proxy is not.

If a proxy is attending, a written and dated authorisation must be shown on demand. Such authorisation can only be given for one year.

It is possible to assign voting rights to others, for example in connection with shareholder agreements, but both irrevocable and revocable assignments can be set aside by the courts where it appears unjust to uphold the assignments.

If the shares serve as security for loans, the transfer of the voting rights must have been expressly agreed.

Protection of Minority Owners

Unanimity is required for decisions whereby:

- the shareholders' rights to profits will be reduced for the benefit of others than the shareholders;
- the shareholders' obligations are to be extended;
- the free transfer of shares is to be limited.

Unless the Internal Rules state that a normal majority suffices, a qualified majority (two thirds of the given votes and of the represented share capital) is required for decisions concerning:

- special changes in the Internal Rules;
- liquidation of the company; and
- transformation into a different form of company.

A general clause in the Act (*Apsl*) seeks to prevent the majority from making decisions favouring some shareholders to the detriment of other shareholders.

An extraordinary general meeting concerning a specific topic can be held when shareholders representing one quarter of the issued capital so request in writing.

Transfer of Ownership

There are no limitations as to transfer of the shares unless otherwise stated in the Internal Rules. Shares can also serve as security for loans. The original shareholder's creditors must be notified about the transfer.

Dissolution/Winding Up

Decisions about dissolution can be made at the general meeting and carried out through liquidation. The Companies Register must be notified about such a decision within 14 days.

A company in the process of liquidation must add to its name that it is in the process of liquidation. The court can appoint one or more liquidators.

The Companies Registrar can decide that a company must be dissolved, as where the company has not submitted the annual accounts in the manner laid down in the Act or where the company does not comply with the rules concerning the management. He will, however, set a time limit enabling the company to comply with the requirements.

Management

The whole board or one member of the board or one executive officer can bind the company. However the Internal Rules may stipulate that a minimum of two or three members is required.

Board (Bestyrelsen)

For companies with a registered capital exceeding DKr 300,000 a board consisting of at least three members is required and the majority of the board members may not be executive officers of the company. Where the capital is less than DKr 300,000 the board can consist of less than three members or no members at all (in the latter case the executive officers will deal with matters normally referred to the board).

The board is elected by the general meeting. The Internal Rules can authorise others (eg local authorities) to appoint one or more members of the board. The board appoints its own chairman. A member of the board or an executive officer can ask for a board meeting to be held.

The minutes of the board meeting must be signed by all attending members. If a board member or an executive officer does not agree with the board's decision, he may require his dissent to be noted. Unless the Internal Rules stipulate a higher attendance, decisions may be taken by a quorum of a majority of the board. Decisions cannot be reached unless all board members have had the possibility of taking part, ie they must have been given notice about the meeting.

At least half the members of the board must be resident in Denmark or in another EC country.

The board members are elected for a period laid down in the Internal Rules (the period cannot exceed four years). Re-election is possible.

The board organises and lays down rules for the day to day management of the company.

Employee Representation (Medarbejderrepræsentation)

Where companies employ more than 35 employees on average over a period of three years, employees may demand representation on the board.

For the employees to obtain board representation a majority of the employees must vote in favour and the board must be notified of this vote in writing. The employees will then be represented by a number equal to one half of the board members already on the board (at least two).

Board members appointed by the employees are appointed for four years.

Employees are eligible for appointment if they have been employed by the company for at least one year.

Executive Officers/Management (Direktion)

The executive officers are appointed by the board. In companies without a board the executive officers are appointed by the general meeting.

An executive officer cannot be appointed chairman of the board.

The executive officers are responsible for the day to day management of the company and must follow the rules and guidelines laid down by the board.

The executive officers' responsibility does not extend to unusual or important decisions without special authorisation from the board. If a decision must be reached before authorisation can be obtained from the board the executive officers must notify the board as soon as possible about the decision.

An executive officer who is not a member of the board can attend the board meetings and is entitled to talk unless the board decides otherwise in each individual case.

Executive officers can bind the company in relation to third parties. The Internal Rules can limit this power by stipulating that a combination of signatures is needed to bind the company.

Executive officers must be resident in Denmark or in another EC country.

Statutory Auditors

In compliance with the Internal Rules one or more statutory auditors are elected by the general meeting.

Statutory auditors are appointed either for a certain number of years or indefinitely. The Internal Rules can authorise others (eg local authorities) to appoint one or more auditors.

At least one of the auditors must be resident in Denmark or in another EC country and at least one of the auditors must be *Statsautoriseret Revisor* (chartered accountant) or *Registreret Revisor*.

When an auditor is to be appointed, shareholders representing at least one quarter of the share capital can require that a *Statsautoriseret Revisor* be appointed.

The following persons cannot be appointed as statutory auditors:

- members of the company's board;
- persons employed by the company or others closely related to the board members or the executive officers;
- family or relatives of the board members or the executive officers.

The auditor is entitled to be present at general meetings and is under a duty to attend the general meetings when the board or a shareholder finds it necessary in relation to financial matters.

Formation Expenses and Taxation

Costs of Registering and Forming a Company

When applying for registration of a new company the following amounts are payable:

- DKr 1,700 plus 0.4 per cent of the subscribed capital;

- one per cent of the registered capital (capital duty).

The above duties will also fall due on additional increases of the share capital.

For registration of changes in company documents the fee is DKr 900.

Costs of Registering a Branch of a Foreign Company
The condition for registering a branch of a foreign company is that the company is registered in its home country.

Upon registration DKr 1,700 plus 0.4 per cent of the foreign company's share capital, with a maximum of DKr 100,000 is payable.

Company Taxation

Resident and Non-Resident Companies
A distinction is made between companies which are incorporated in accordance with Danish company law (and thus deemed to be resident) and non-resident companies (eg a branch of a foreign company). An incorporated company is resident irrespective of where the activities are carried out and where the management is situated.

The worldwide income of a resident company will be subject to Danish taxation.

A non-resident company will be subject to Danish taxation in relation to income accruing from land, royalties, dividends and also profits from permanent establishments.

Companies are not subject to capital gains tax of profits, but capital gains will be subject to company income tax.

Examples of gains exempt from income tax are:

- shares held for at least three years;
- buildings owned for more than seven years;
- bonds and debentures bought at a special discount;
- sale of goodwill.

Tax Rates
The income tax rate for both resident and non-resident companies is 50 per cent.

Thirty per cent tax is withheld on distributions from a Danish company.

Tax is withheld in relation to employee remuneration, royalties and dividends. This is subject to the rules following from the tax treaties entered into.

Taxable Income
The gross income may be redefined by:

- deductions (all expenses related to current income);
- write-down of inventories (up to 30 per cent of either the cost or replacement value);
- business expenses (expenses related to current income);
- allocation to investment funds (up to 25 per cent of the taxable income. The investment fund must be used within six years of the year of allocation. Normally it will be required to deposit, in a blocked bank account, the equivalent of 50 per cent of the deduction);
- certain relief provisions applicable in relation to income from foreign sources (amounting to 50 per cent on the net taxable income of foreign entities if a resident company is jointly taxed with subsidiaries).

Losses may be carried forward for five years but cannot be carried back.

Declining balance depreciation is possible on machinery, equipment, vehicles and ships at maximum 25 per cent in the first year of acquisition and maximum 30 per cent in the following years.

Straight-line depreciation is allowed on buildings used for commercial purposes (except office purposes).

Fundamental Legislative Texts

Laws
Anpartsselskabsloven (Apsl), Lovbekendtg 1985-11-15 nr 484 as amended by *L 1986-06-04 nr 317 and 324 and L1987-06-10 nr 384 and 401 and L1987-12-23 nr 851.*

- *Lov 1981-06-10 nr 284 om visse selskabers aflæggelse af årsregnskab mv;*
- *Lov 1985-03-31 nr 128 om begraensning af tantieme og vederlag mv;*
- *Lov 1973-5-23 nr 284 om kapitaltilførelsesafgifter* as amended by *L Bek 1975-12-10 nr 604* as amended by *L Bek 1976-04-28 nr 216* as amended by *L Bek 1978-05-03 nr 193;*

51

- *Lovbekendtg 1986-9-22 nr 658 om indkomstbeskatning af aktieselskaber mv.*

Decrees

Bekendtg 1977-02-24 nr 64 om udenlandske aktieselskabers og anpartsselskabers adgang til at oprette filialer.

- *Bekendtg 1977-02-24 nr 63 om fravigelse af bopælskrav mv i aktieselskabsloven og anpartsselskabsloven;*
- *Bekendtg 1986-12-17 nr 967 om anmeldelser mv til aktieselskabs-registeret for aktie- og anpartsselskaber;*
- *Bekendtg 1985-04-18 om aktieselskabs-registerets takster for aktie- og anpartsselskaber;*
- *Bekendtg 1982-12-03 nr 611 om indsendelse og offentliggørelse af årsregnskaber mv;*
- *Bekendtg 1985-03-31 nr 129 om kontrol med beregning af tantieme og vederlag mv.*

PUBLIC COMPANY

(Aktieselskaber)

Documents

Memorandum and Articles of Association (Stiftelsesdokument)
Stiftelsesdokumentet is one document in two parts constituting both the memorandum and articles of association. To avoid confusion the two parts of the document are referred to as Internal Rules (*Vedtægter*) and General Information. The memorandum and articles of association as a whole will be referred to as *Stiftelsesdokumentet*.

Internal Rules
The contents must specify:

- the company's name and, if applicable, any additional names;
- the county where the head office of the company is to be located;
- the purpose of the company;
- the amount of capital to be paid in to the company with a minimum of DKr 300,000. For the period of time until the first general meeting it will suffice to state the minimum amount to be subscribed and the maximum amount that can be subscribed;
- the nominal amount of the shares and the shareholders' voting rights;
- the term of office and the minimum and maximum number of board members and possible substitutes;
- the term of office and the minimum and maximum number of statutory auditors and possible substitutes;
- the procedure for calling general meetings;
- what issues may be taken up by general meetings;
- the fiscal year;
- whether the shares are to be issued to a name or to the bearer;
- whether the shares are not to be for order.

When applicable the following must also be specified:

- a duty for the shareholders to let the company or others take over their shares in part or wholly;

- any limitations as to the transfer of shares;
- special rights for certain shares;
- limitations in the subscription rights for board members and executive officers;
- whether it has been decided to have a management consisting of three or more members and if so the minimum and maximum amount of executive officers.

General Information

The contents must include:

- the promoters' names, titles and addresses;
- the subscription price for the shares;
- time limits for the subscription and the payment of the shares;
- the period of time before the constituting general meeting is to be held and in which way the general meeting must be called unless the general meeting is to be held without being called;
- whether the company is to pay the costs incurred at the formation and if so to which extent. These costs must be specified.

The following information must also be provided together with a statement from the statutory auditor as to its accuracy:

- whether payment in kind may be made and if so, the valuation thereof (the payment in kind must be some kind of property and it must have an economic value but it cannot consist of a duty to provide services or work);
- whether the company is to take over such payment in exchange for shares;
- whether promoters or others will be given special rights or benefits; and
- whether special agreements, which will financially burden the company, are to be made with promoters or others.

If the company in formation is taking over an existing company an opening balance must be made by the statutory auditor and this must be enclosed.

The subscription of shares must either be incorporated in *Stiftelsesdokumentet* or on share lists containing a complete copy of *Stiftelsesdokumentet*. The subscription of shares must be without conditions.

Shares must be issued within one year of the registration of the share subscription. The shares must not be distributed until registration has taken place and the shares have been fully paid for. Shares issued to a name must not be handed out until they have been noted in the list of shareholders.

The shares must contain the name of the company, the address of the company, its registration number and the nominal value of the share. The shares must be signed by the board (can be done mechanically).

Minute Book (Forhandlingsprotokollen)

Summaries of general meetings are kept in the minute book which is signed by the presiding chairman. The minute book or a copy thereof must be available for the shareholders for inspection at the company's office no longer than 14 days after the general meeting.

Accounting Books (Årsregnskab)

The annual accounts must consist of the following:

- a balance (Balance/Status);
- a profit and loss statement (Resultatopgørelse);
- notes (Noter);
- an annual report (Årsberetning).

For parent companies the consolidated accounts of all subsidiaries are also required.

Registration Form (Registreringsanmeldelsesblanket)

The forms for registration can be obtained from the local police station.

The information to be submitted must at least mention:

- the company's name and address and also a postal address if different;
- the company's first financial year;
- the amount of capital raised, the amount paid in, the form of payment, the nominal amount of shares not fully paid, and when the remainder must be paid;
- the full name, title and address of the promoter(s), board members, executive officers, auditors and of any substitutes.

The form must be accompanied by:

- Stiftelsesdokumentet and other documents relating to the formation (either the original or in copy certified by the board). Documents relating to the formation include conveyance deeds, leasing contracts, licensing contracts and any other relevant documents of this kind;

- a certified extract of the minutes from the constituting general meeting;
- evidence that at least two of the promoters are either resident in Denmark or are resident in another EC Member State;
- evidence that board members, executive officers and auditors are 18 years old or over and in good standing. It must be shown that all executive officers and at least half of the board members are Danish residents or EC residents and that one or more of the auditors is a Danish resident and either *Stats-autoriseret Revisor* or *Registreret Revisor*.
- evidence that the persons certifying the correctness of the information given in *Stiftelsesdokumentet* are 18 years old or over and of good standing.
- evidence of payment of at least one half of the capital — and at least DKr 300,000 — has been paid in.

The application form must be signed by all board members. The signatures must be certified by a notary, an *Advokat* or by two witnesses. The documents must be in Danish.

Registration Requirements

Trade and Industry
Application must be made on a form obtainable from the local police station and must when completed be sent to the Companies Register (*Erhverus- og Selskabsstyrelsen*) at the following address:

Erhverus- og Selskabsstyrelsen
Kampmannsgade 1
1604 Copenhagen V.

The board must apply for registration within six months of the date of *Stiftelsesdokumentet*. Registration will be refused if the six months period is exceeded.

The company is given a number when registered.

All registrations are immediately made public in *Statstidende*. Information made public in *Statstidende* is deemed to be known by third parties, with certain exceptions.

Tax Authority

Companies with employees must register with the local Inland Revenue (*Skattemyndighederne*) at the register called *Arbejdsgiverregisteret*. Forms are obtainable from the local Inland Revenue Office.

VAT Authority

Companies must furthermore register with the Customs Officer (*Toldvæsenet*) to be placed on the VAT Register (*Momsregisteret*). Forms can be obtained from the local Customs Office.

Capital Requirements

Minimum Amount

The minimum authorised, issued and paid up capital is DKr 300,000. At least three shares must be issued.

The capital must have been subscribed and distributed among the participants and at least half of the capital, this not being less than DKr 300,000 in addition to any amounts paid for the share in excess of the face value, must be paid in.

The remainder must be paid within a year after registration of the company.

The amount payable for a share must not be lower than the nominal amount of the share.

Type of Capital Paid In

Payment of the capital must actually be made. Payment is made when the control over the money or assets constituting the payment has moved from the shareholder to the company.

Payment can be made in kind but it must be property with an economic value. It cannot consist of a duty to provide services or work.

Limits to Liability

The shareholders are not personally liable (that is with all their own assets) for the obligations of the company. Joint liability will, however, be imposed for obligations entered into before registration of the company.

Registration of the the company results in a transfer of obligations to the company. These obligations must either have been mentioned in *Stiftelsesdokumentet* or have been incurred after the signing of *Stiftelsesdokumentet*.

57

Liability will be imposed on shareholders for intentional or negligent acts. The damages can be reduced under circumstances where it appears to be just to do so. If several persons are liable they will be liable jointly and severally.

Ownership

Type of Ownership

The participants in an *Aktieselskab* are shareholders (*Aktionærer*). A minimum of three shares must be issued and at least three promoters are required.

Voting Rights

All shares give equal rights in the company, unless otherwise stated in the Internal Rules.

The shareholder can authorise a proxy to attend the general meeting on his behalf. Only the shareholder is entitled to bring an adviser, a proxy is not.

If a proxy is attending a written and dated authorisation must be shown on demand. Such authorisation can only be given for one year.

It is possible to assign voting rights to others, for example in connection with shareholder agreements, but both irrevocable and revocable assignments can be set aside by the courts where it appears unjust to uphold the assignments.

If the shares serve as security for loans, the transfer of the voting rights must have been expressly agreed.

Protection of Minority Owners

Unanimity is required for decisions whereby:

- the shareholders' rights to profits are to be reduced for the benefit of others than the shareholders;
- the shareholders' obligations are to be extended;
- the free transfer of shares is to be limited.

A qualified majority (two-thirds of the given votes and of the represented share capital) is required for decisions concerning:

- special changes in the Internal Rules;
- liquidation of the company;
- transformation.

A general clause in the Act seeks to prevent the majority from making decisions favouring some shareholders to the detriment of other shareholders.

An extraordinary general meeting concerning a specific topic can be held when shareholders representing one tenth of the issued capital so requests in writing.

Transfer of Ownership

There are no limitations as to the transfer of shares.

The shares can be nominative or bearer. For nominative shares the Internal Rules can stipulate limitations on transferability.

The company can be listed on the stock exchange. For a company listed on the stock exchange one of the statutory auditors must be a chartered accountant (*Statsautoriseret Revisor*). Before the shares can be listed a prospectus as regards to the company's financial situation must be published.

The companies are divided into three groups for the purpose of listing: groups I and II require the company's capital to be at least DKr 15m, whereas listing under group III requires the capital to be between DKr 2m and 15m.

For a company to be listed it can be required that a certain amount of shares must be offered for sale to the public, thus listing under group III requires that at least 15 per cent of the capital and not less than DKr 1m must be offered for sale.

Dissolution/Winding Up

Decisions about dissolution can be made at the general meeting and carried out through liquidation. The Companies Register must be notified about the decision within 14 days.

A company in the process of liquidation must add to its name that it is in the process of liquidation. The court can appoint one or more liquidators.

The Companies Registrar can decide that a company must be dissolved, as where the company has not submitted the annual accounts in the manner laid down in the Act or where the company does not comply with the rules concerning the mamagement. He will, however, set a time limit enabling the company to comply with the requirements.

Management

The whole board or one member of the board or one executive officer can bind the company. However the Internal Rules may stipulate that a minimum of two or three members is required.

Board (Bestyrelsen)

The company must have a board consisting of at least three members.

It can be decided in the Internal Rules that a board of specially appointed representatives is to be elected by the general meeting.

The board is elected by the General Meeting unless the Internal Rules states that the board of representatives is to appoint the board.

The Internal Rules can authorise others (eg local authorities) to appoint one or more members of the board.

The majority of the board members may not be executive officers in the company.

The board appoints its own chairman.

A member of the board or an executive officer can ask for a board meeting to be held.

The minutes of the board meeting must be signed by all attending members. If a board member or an executive officer does not agree with the board's decision, he may require his dissent to be noted.

Unless the Internal Rules stipulate a higher attendance, decisions may be taken by a quorum of a majority of the board. Decisions cannot be reached unless all board members have had the possibility of taking part, ie they must have been given notice about the meeting.

At least half the members of the board must be resident in Denmark or in another EC country. The board members are elected for a period laid down in the Internal Rules, maximum four years. Re-election is possible. The board organises and lays down rules for the day to day management of the company.

The board of representatives must consist of at least five members. The Internal Rules must contain provisions relating to the board of representatives. The task of the board of representatives is to ensure that the board and the executive officers administer the company in accordance with the rules.

The board of representatives can call for an extraordinary general meeting to be held and if laid down in the Internal Rules, the representatives can appoint the board and fix the board members' remuneration.

Employee representation (Medarbejderrepræsentation)

Where companies employ more than 35 employees on average over a period of three years, employees may demand representation on the board.

For the employees to obtain board representation a majority of the employees must vote in favour and the board must be notified of this vote in writing. The employees will then be represented by a number equal to one half of the board members already on the board (at least two).

Board members appointed by the employees are appointed for four years.

Employees are eligible for appointment if they have been employed with the company for at least one year.

Executive Officers/Management (Direktion)

The board appoints one to three executive officers unless the Internal Rules require a greater number.

An executive officer cannot be appointed chairman of the board.

The executive officers are responsible for the day to day management of the company and must follow the rules and guidelines laid down by the board.

The executive officers' responsibility does not extend to unusual or important decisions without special authorisation from the board. If a decision must be reached before authorisation can be obtained from the board the executive officers must notify the board as soon possible.

An executive officer who is not a member of the board can attend the board meetings and is entitled to participate unless the board decides otherwise in each individual case.

Executive officers can bind the company in relation to third parties. The Internal Rules can limit this power by stipulating that a combination of signatures is needed to bind the company.

Executive officers must be resident in Denmark or in another EC country.

Statutory Auditors

In compliance with the Internal Rules one or more statutory auditors are elected at the general meeting.

Statutory auditors are appointed either for a certain number of years or indefinitely. The Internal Rules can authorise others (local authorities) to appoint one or more auditors.

At least one of the auditors must be resident in Denmark or in another EC country.

At least one of the auditors must be *Statsautoriseret Revisor* (chartered accountant) or *Registreret Revisor*.

In companies listed on the stock exchange two auditors must be elected and at least one of them must be a *Statsautoriseret Revisor*.

When an auditor is to be appointed shareholders representing at least one tenth of the share capital can require that a *Statsautoriseret Revisor* be appointed.

The following persons cannot be appointed as statutory auditors:

- members of the company's board;
- persons employed by the company or others closely related to the board members or to the executive officers;
- family or relatives of the board members or the executive officers.

The auditor is entitled to be present at general meetings and is under a duty to attend the general meetings when the board or a shareholder finds it necessary in relation to financial matters.

Formation Expenses and Taxation

Costs of Registering and Forming a Company

When applying for registration of a new company the following amounts are payable:

- DKr 1,700 plus 0.4 per cent of the subscribed capital
- one per cent of the registered capital (capital duty).

The above duties will also fall due on additional increases of the share capital.

For registration of changes in company documents the fee is DKr 900.

Costs of Registering a Branch of a Foreign Company

The condition for registering a branch of a foreign company is that the company is registered in its home country.

Upon registration DKr 1,700 plus 0.4 per cent of the foreign company's share capital, with a maximum of Dkr 100,000 is payable.

Company Taxation:

Resident and Non-Resident Companies:

A distinction is made between companies which are incorporated in accordance with Danish company law (and thus deemed to be resident) and non-resident companies (eg a branch of a foreign company). An incorporated company is resident irrespective of where the activities are carried out and where the management is situated.

The worldwide income of a resident company will be subject to Danish taxation.

A non-resident company will be subject to Danish taxation in relation to income accruing from land, royalties, dividends and also profits from permanent establishments.

Companies are not subject to capital gains tax of profits, however the capital gains will be subject to company income tax.

Examples of gains exempt from income tax are:

- shares held for at least three years;
- buildings owned for more than seven years;
- bonds and debentures bought at a special discount;
- sale of goodwill.

Tax Rates
The income tax rate for both resident and non-resident companies is 50 per cent.

Thirty per cent tax is withheld on distributions from a Danish company.

Tax is withheld in relation to employee remuneration, royalties and dividends. This is subject to the rules following from the tax treaties entered into.

Taxable Income
The gross income may be redefined by:

- deductions (all expenses related to current income);
- write-down of inventories (up to 30 per cent of either the cost or replacement value);
- business expenses (expenses related to current income);
- allocation to investment funds (up to 25 per cent of the taxable income. The investment fund must be used within six years of the year of allocation. Normally it will be required to deposit, in a blocked bank account, the equivalent of 50 per cent of the deduction);
- certain relief provisions applicable in relation to income from foreign sources (amounting to 50 per cent on the net taxable income of foreign entities if a resident company is jointly taxed with subsidiaries).

Losses may be carried forward for five years but cannot be carried back.

Declining balance depreciation is possible on machinery, equipment, vehicles and ships at maximum 25 per cent in the first year of acquisition and maximum 30 per cent in the following years.

Straight-line depreciation is allowed on buildings used for commercial purposes (except office purposes).

Fundamental Legislative Texts

Laws

Aktieselskabsloven (Asl) Lovbekendtg. 1985-11-15 nr 283 as amended by *L 1986-06-04 nr 317, 318 and 324 and L1987-06-10 nr 384 and 401 and L1987-12-23 nr 851.*

- *Lov 1981-06-10 nr 284 om visse selskabers aflæggelse af årsregnskab mv;*
- *Lov 1985-03-31 nr 128 om begrænsning af tantieme og vederlag mv;*
- *Lov 1973-5-23 nr 284 om kapitaltilførselsafgifter* as amended by *L Bek 1975-12-10 nr 604* as amended by *L Bek 1976-04-28 nr 216* as amended by *L Bek 1978-05-03 nr 193;*
- *L Bek 1986-9-22 nr 658 om indkomstbeskatning af aktieselskaber mv;*
- *Lov 1972-6-7 nr 220 om Københavns Fondsbørs* with amendments;
- *L Bek. 1983-11-10 nr 525 om Københavns Fondsbørs,* as amended by *L Bek nr 526, 527 and 528 all 1983-11-10.*

Decrees

Bekendtg 1977-02-24 nr 64 om udenlandske aktieselskabers og anpartsselskabers adgang til at oprette filialer.

- *Bekendtg 1977-02-24 nr 63 om fravigelse af bopælskrav mv i aktieselskabsloven og anpartsselskabsloven;*
- *Bekendtg 1986-12-17 nr 967 om anmeldelser mv til aktieselskabs-registeret for aktie- og anpartsselskaber;*
- *Bekendtg 1985-04-18 om aktieselskabs-registerets takster for aktie- og anpartsselskaber;*
- *Bekendtg 1982-12-03 nr 611 om indsendelse og offentliggørelse af årsregnskaber mv;*
- *Bekendtg 1985-03-31 nr 129 om kontrol med beregning af tantieme og vederlag mv.*

FRANCE

PRIVATE COMPANY
(Société à Responsabilité Limitée)

PUBLIC COMPANY
(Société Anonyme)

INTRODUCTION

In France, the law of 24 July 1966 provides for a variety of company types. The two most important forms are the *Société Anonyme* (SA) and the *Société à Responsabilité Limitée* (SARL). The primary distinction between the two is that equity in the SA is not usually restricted to the founders of the company, while the equity of the SARL is closely held.

There are two types of SA, quoted and unquoted. The former has negotiable shares or debentures quoted on the French stock exchange (*Bourse*) and offered for sale to the general public. The latter, though privately owned, is a hybrid, corresponding closely to the publicly held company for most purposes.

It is possible to incorporate a quoted SA by making a public offering of shares to raise the initial registered capital. This method of incorporation is very rare within a French domestic context. The normal procedure is that another form of company is transformed into the 'public' SA. Therefore this work will deal with unquoted SAs only.

Perhaps confusingly, there are two types of management structures available to either kind of SA, a typical board of directors and a rather informal supervisory council. A board of directors is usual for a public (quoted) SA.

A privately held (unquoted) SA requires a minimum capital of F 250,000. In contrast, the minimum capital is F 1,500,000 for a quoted company. Shares must have a par value closely reflecting the real value of the shares, and it is rare, though quite possible, for preferred or restricted stock to be issued.

The other type of limited liability company is unknown in the UK and the USA. The SARL is well suited to 'family' businesses, with an informal management structure, a limited number of members (*associés*) who may own equity, a low capital requirement (F 50,000) and the ability to establish the successors by inheritance of the company founders in the original agreement.

Company formation in France is somewhat rigid in preventing the development of 'off the shelf' registration. However, transformations from one type of company structure to another are allowed and provide the flexibility otherwise lacking in this area.

PRIVATE COMPANY

(Société à Responsabilité Limitée)

Documents

Memorandum and Articles of Association (Les Statuts)
In France, the memorandum and articles of association are contained in the same document setting up a limited liability company (SARL), *Les Statuts*, henceforth referred to as the articles or articles of incorporation.

Mandatory Provisions
- declaration that the members associate themselves by forming a SARL;
- the name of the SARL;
- duration of the SARL (maximum 99 years);
- address of the registered office;
- statement specifying the purpose of the SARL. Certain activities may not be carried out by a SARL: insurance, capitalisation, savings;
- declaration of the amount of registered capital;
- enumeration of the identity and equity holdings of each member.

An amendment is necessary whenever equity is transferred.

Optional Provisions
- method of appointment of the company officer(s) (*gérant*);
- enumeration of the powers of the company officer(s);
- rules governing sale, transfer or assignment of equity;
- rules governing decisions of members;
- fixing of the fiscal year;
- rules governing liquidation.

Required Annexes
A recital of all contracts entered into and of the commitments and obligations assumed by the founding members in the name of the company, before signature of the articles.

Minute Book
A minute book (*registre des procès-verbaux*) must be set up on special numbered paper, stamped by a judge of the Commercial Court, for the minutes of the shareholders' meetings.

Accounting Books
Immediately after registration in the Register of Commerce and Companies (*Registre du Commerce et des Sociétés*), the SARL must set up accounting books according to the accountancy standard (*plan comptable*) laid down by the fiscal regulations of the Minister of Finance.

Registration Requirements

Introduction
Apart from filing a declaration with various government departments (Finance, Social Security, etc), every commercial undertaking in France must be registered at the Register of Commerce and Corporations and notice of formation must be made known to the public.

Failure to comply with registration requirements will result in civil and penal sanctions, the latter in the form of fines and/or prison sentences. The most important civil sanction will be the absence of legal personality, preventing the 'company' from carrying on business with third parties in the name of the company.

Formalities of Formation

Prior to the Signing of the Articles
Cash contributions must be subscribed and fully paid up to one of the promoters, whose deposit of funds with an approved third party, either a bank, a notary, or a governmental deposit and consignment office, must be evidenced.

Contributions in kind must be valued by the contribution auditor (*commissaire aux apports*) appointed by the Commercial Court. This valuation report must be attached to the annex of the articles.

The report of the contribution auditor is not obligatory if the decision not to use one is unanimous, if each contribution does not exceed F 50,000, and if the total amount of these contributions does not exceed one half of the capital subscribed.

Signing of the Articles by all the Members
The articles may be signed with an ordinary, unwitnessed signature (*sous seing privé*) or before a notary. However, when contributions in

the form of rights to real property are made, signature before a notary is mandatory.

Procedure Subsequent to the Signing of the Articles

Filing of Articles of Incorporation with the tax authorities
The articles must be filed within one month from the date of the last signature (*art 635-1-5 du Code Général des Impôts*) at the office of the relevant tax authorities, ie either where the registered office is located or at the home address of one of the promoters.

Notice of formation
Notice of formation must be made in a journal specifically designated as competent to publish legal announcements; a list of suitable journals is published by the local administrative authorities (*préfecture*).

This notice must state the type of company, amount of share capital, registered office, objects of the company and the type of capital contributions.

Declaration of conformity
This is a declaration that the company has been formed in accord with applicable law. It is a deed (document) detailing the proposed operation of the company, certifying that the shares have been subscribed and fully paid up. It must be signed in triplicate by all the shareholders and filed in the Register of Commerce and Companies along with the articles of incorporation.

Registration of documents
The documents must be lodged at the 'Formalities Centre' (*Centre Unique des Formalités*), located in the local Chamber of Commerce. Since 1981 these Formalities Centres have served as clearing houses, receiving all the necessary documentation and transmitting it thereafter to the various departments such as the Register of Commerce and Companies, the Commercial Court, the tax authorities etc. However, if any difficulties arise, they are resolved directly with the authority concerned.

The registration file must contain

- two copies of the articles;
- two copies of the deeds nominating the manager and the statutory auditor (if this has been done);

- two copies of the declaration of conformity;
- report of the contribution auditor;
- application for registration — indicating all the different elements of the identity of the company);
- a copy of the request for notice to be published in the legal journal;
- documents proving the identity and the commercial capacity of the managers and auditors;
- documents verifying the type of the contributions in kind, and the identity of the contributor.

Official registration

Once all the necessary checks are completed, the clerk of the Commercial Court provides the identification number of the company, which is registered at the Register of Commerce and Companies. He then arranges for the publication of a notice in the *Bulletin Officiel des Annonces Civiles et Commerciales*.

This number must be used in all correspondence with official authorities and must appear on the company letterhead, invoices, and all other company documentation.

The effective date of registration is the date of lodgement of the papers with the application for registration, so long as the clerk of the Commercial Court has not made any objection or refusal within 15 days of that date.

Withdrawal of funds

Capital subscriptions paid in cash will only be released for the company's use when the registration certificate is obtained and presented.

Publication of contributions in kind

Publication of the transfer of property and business forming the basis of contributions in kind must be completed as soon as possible in order that the transfer to the company may be effective as against third parties. This is usually the responsibility of the notary who completes the transfer deeds.

Administrative responsibilities

A *déclaration d'existence*, sent to the tax and social security authorities, must be filled out when applying for registration at the Formalities Centre.

Capital Requirements

Minimum Amounts

The minimum legal capital of a SARL is F 50,000. This capital takes the form of non-negotiable, nominal certificates of equity (*parts social*) of equal amounts, with a minimum value of F 100. These are participations in capital as evidenced by written deed. The SARL may not issue negotiable equity certificates or make public offerings of its equity.

Type of Capital Paid In

The capital must be fully subscribed, issued and paid either in cash (*apport en espèces*), or in kind (*apport en nature*) at the time of incorporation. When payment is made in kind, the evaluation by the *commissaire aux apports*, who is an independent appraiser appointed by the Commercial Court, must be incorporated into the articles. Equity subscribers making 'in kind' contributions are liable for five years to third parties for the appraised value of these contributions.

Ownership

Composition of Ownership

A SARL may be created by two or more equity holders or members, who may be legal entities, French nationals, or foreign nationals, with a maximum membership of 50. A SARL that has more than 50 members must be transformed into an SA or wound up within two years.

Voting Rights

A right to vote at general and extraordinary meetings of the company attaches inalienably to each share. Each owner has a number of votes directly proportional to the equity held. There is no non-voting or preferential equity. Decisions may be made at a meeting of the owners or by written consultation.

Any provision in the articles of association purporting to restrict participation in members' meetings, for example to a minimum equity holding, is void.

An equity holder may only be represented at a meeting of the members by another member or his spouse unless the articles of association otherwise provide, unless such other member or spouse is the only other member of the company. In general, the authority to represent a member may only be given to the representative for one meeting (or for two meetings where these are a general and extraordinary meeting held within seven days of each other).

Member's Meetings

Members have the right 15 days before the annual obligatory general meeting to receive the company officer's report, the profit and loss account, the annual accounts, the texts of proposed resolutions and, if relevant, the auditor's report. The annual general meeting must take place within six months after the end of the relevant accounting year.

A members' meeting is compulsory within the four months following an annual auditor's report stating that the capital assets of the company have fallen below 50 per cent of the amount of its registered nominal capital (to decide whether or not to voluntarily wind up the company); or where the number of members has surpassed 50.

Members' meetings are presided over by a company officer or one of the company officers, or the member with the greatest number of votes present.

Ordinary general meetings of the members are necessary to approve the accounts, to fix dividends, to remove and appoint company officers, to fix their remuneration, to approve contracts between the company and the company officers and to authorise the company officers to carry out functions which exceed the company officers' powers as set out in the articles of incorporation.

These decisions are taken by one or more of the members representing more than 50 per cent of the shares (*la majorité absolue*). Failure to meet this condition will result in a second vote the outcome of which will be determined by a simple majority (*une majorité relative*) unless otherwise stated in the articles of incorporation.

Extraordinary general meetings of the members must be held for the purposes of authorising the subscription of equity in the company by non-members or of amending the memorandum and articles of incorporation, but not to transform the SARL into an SA with capital assets of less than F 5,000,000, or to remove a company officer.

Decisions to change the nationality of the company or to require a member to increase his capital contribution, including the transformation of a SARL into a partnership (*société en nom collectif*) or limited partnership (*société en commandite*) require unanimity on the part of the members.

Decisions to sell or pledge shares in the company to outsiders requires the agreement of a majority of the members *and* a majority of members representing three quarters of the shares.

A decision removing a company officer from office requires only a simple majority. Other decisions to modify the articles of incorporation require a majority of members representing three quarters of the shares.

Protection of Minority Owners

One or more members have the right to convene a meeting of the company's members if they own 50 per cent of the equity or, if holding at least one quarter of the equity, they represent at least a quarter of the members of the company.

Every member may seek the appointment by the court of a representative to call and fix the agenda for a meeting of the members. Under normal circumstances, this task falls to the company officer when he considers it appropriate. The members may require the inclusion of one item on the agenda and require an answer in the meeting of a reply to their written questions.

Members have the right at all times to examine the annual accounts of the company, inventories, company officer's reports, auditor's reports, minutes of meetings and reports submitted to members' meetings. They may also address two written questions each annual accounting period to the company officer.

Where the annual meeting refuses to distribute dividends, the minority owners may seek an action in nullity for abuse of power.

Transfer of Ownership

All transfers of equity must be made by written deed.

Equity may not be sold to non-members of the company unless the consent of a three-quarters majority of the members is first obtained. Equity is freely transferable between the members and may be transferred to spouses and legatees or heirs of members in the case of death or divorce unless otherwise specified in the articles of incorporation.

Where a shareholder wishes to withdraw from the company, the other members must either buy the retiring shareholder's shares or reduce the capital of the company. Their failure to do so will enable the retiring member to sell his shares to an outsider.

Dissolution/Winding Up

If a SARL, due to financial difficulties, is unable to pay its creditors, the Commercial Court may be petitioned to take whatever action is necessary by a creditor, a shareholder or the State Prosecutor.

The Court may order a period of observation which may last up to two years. All normal business (except the mortgaging of assets) of the SARL may continue during this period. A receiver, a creditor's representative and an employee representative will be appointed by the Court.

If after this period, the receiver decides that the financial difficulties cannot be solved, a bankruptcy (*liquidation des biens*) will be recommended. If the Court agrees with this decision, the SARL will be wound up. If a solution is deemed possible a reconstruction plan must be submitted to the Court. If approved, this plan is implemented under the supervision of parties appointed by the Court.

Dissolution of the SARL will occur for reasons such as the end of its period of duration, achievement of purpose, decision of its shareholders, court decision.

If the registered capital falls below F 50,000, the SARL must, within one year, increase its capital or transform into another form of company.

If the value of the assets of the SARL falls below one half of its registered capital, an extraordinary general meeting must decide whether to dissolve the company or to remedy the situation.

If the number of shareholders exceeds 50, the SARL must, within two years, reduce the number of shareholders or transform into another form of company. Otherwise the company is automatically dissolved.

Management

As the membership of a SARL is limited, there is no requirement for a board or council representing the owners to supervise the company officers. Such functions are performed by meetings of all the members.

Company Officers

A SARL is managed by one or more company officers, who must be physical persons. They do not have to own any part of the SARL.

There is no statutory provision which requires the company officers to hold formal meetings among themselves.

A company officer who is not an EC citizen (and has no resident's card) must obtain a commercial card (*carte de commerçant*).

The articles of incorporation will usually name one or more company officers; they may also be elected by a majority vote based on ownership.

It is common practice to appoint the company officer(s) for a limited period of time, such as one year, because their removal without cause may make the company subject to liability to the individual director(s).

Save when otherwise provided for in the articles, each company officer has the right to act independently of the other(s) to bind the SARL *vis à vis* third parties.

Statutory Auditors

A statutory auditor and an alternate statutory auditor (*Suppléant*) must be appointed by the owners for all SARLs that, at the end of a fiscal year, satisfy two of the following three criteria:

- net value of the assets over F 10,000,000;
- pre-tax turnover greater than F 20,000,000;
- more than 50 employees.

Formation Expenses and Taxation

Costs of Registering and Forming a Company

These costs are exactly the same as those for the formation of the SA.

Publication in the official journal: approximately F 1,500. Commercial registration expenses: F 1,300. Stamp taxes: approximately F 1,000.

Capital Taxes

It is necessary to distinguish between *capital contributions* (payments to the company in exchange for shares in that company) where the subscriber becomes a member of the company and *capital additions* (additions to the fixed or current capital assets of a company, creating a matching liability) where the contributor becomes a creditor of the company.

Capital Contributions

A distinction must be made depending on the tax paying position of the subscriber.

For a contribution from a party who is subject to corporation tax, the tax on the contribution will be 1 per cent in respect of all types of contributions.

Contributions from parties not subject to corporation tax are taxed as follows:

Cash contributions
— subscriptions in cash, capital additions, and personal (movable) property are all considered as cash contributions. Tax rate: 1 per cent.

Contributions in kind
— these include real property, rights in real property, goodwill or interest in a business. Tax rate: 11.4 per cent plus local taxes payable on real property (see below).

Capital Additions
These are subject to the same tax regime as is relevant to the transfer of the particular property or asset which form the basis of the contribution, the most common of which are the following:

Real property
— generally the rate is 16.6 per cent (plus various local taxes depending on the different regions – 0.5 per cent to 1.6 per cent) but this is subject to numerous exceptions.

Transfer of a business (in whole or in part)
— generally the rate is 16.6 per cent but again this is subject to numerous exceptions.

Transfer of stock on hand
— the tax imposed in this instance is the VAT applicable to the particular goods being transferred.

Corporate Income Tax
The corporate income tax is fixed at 45 per cent on taxable income with a minimum fixed periodically by decree. Currently the minimum varies between F 4,000 and F 17,000 depending on the taxpayer's turnover.

Fundamental Legislative Texts

- Code Civil, art. 1832 through 1844-17
- Decree No 78-704 of 3 July 1978
- Law No 66-537 of 24 July 1966
- Decree No 67-236 of 23 March 1967
- Decree No 84-406 of 30 May 1984
- Regulation of 24 September 1984
- Circular of 24 October 1985

PUBLIC COMPANY

(Société Anonyme)

Documents

Memorandum and Articles of Association (Les Statuts)
In France, these may be prepared by the future members or their advisers and there is no requirement for a notary to authenticate the signatures.

The articles may contain as many provisions as the directors require but must supply the following minimal information:

- name of company and declaration of intention to form a SA;
- duration – this cannot exceed 99 years;
- address of the registered office;
- objects of the SA — this must be a specific recital of the nature of the proposed activity of the enterprise;
- amount of registered capital;
- the identity of the founding members and the number of shares for which each has subscribed;
- declaration of the number of shares and their par value and specific mention of different classes of shares if any;
- provisions relating to the distribution of profits and priorities in a liquidation;
- appointment of the first members of the board of directors and the statutory auditor;
- provisions detailing the composition, function and powers of the directors and the auditor;
- details of all contracts entered into and commitments and obligations assumed by the founding shareholders in the name of the SA before formation must be attached to the articles;

Company Books
Immediately after registration in the Register of Companies, the SA is required to maintain accounting books, certain of which must be on special numbered paper stamped by the Commercial Court (*Tribunal de Commerce*). These books include a general journal, a

general ledger and an inventory ledger. Other compulsory books include an attendance book (for the board of directors), minute books (for shareholders and directors' meetings — these must be on a special register and each page must be initialled) and a stock transfer book.

Registration Requirements

The procedure relating to the registration of an SA is the same as that for the SARL except that before signing, a draft of the articles must be prepared and lodged at the future registered office.

Also, if there are to be capital contributions in kind, a contribution auditor (*commissaire aux apports*) must be appointed and his valuation report annexed to, and approved at the same time as, the articles.

All the shares must be fully subscribed and 25 per cent of their par value deposited with an approved depositary (bank, notary, deposit and consignment office) which will prepare a certificate of subscription subsequent to the deposit.

A list must be prepared of all pre-incorporation acts carried out by the promoters, which will be attached to the articles as an annex. The final draft of the articles will then be prepared and delivered to the shareholders.

Signature of the Articles by all Shareholders
This procedure is identical to that for a SARL.

Procedure Subsequent to the Signing of the Articles
This procedure is identical to that for a SARL.

Capital Requirements

Minimum Amounts
An SA must have a minimum subscribed capital, of F 250,000 and shares must be issued with a minimum par value of F 100.

Original shares in an SA are allotted in the articles of incorporation signed by the subscribers. Contributions subscribed for an SA must be unconditional, of real value, and in cash or in kind.

Types of Capital Paid In
Shares may be paid for with cash or in kind contributions.

An SA may issue negotiable debentures once it has been in existence for two years, the capital has been fully paid up and the financial statements have been approved by the shareholders for two fiscal years.

Liability of Subscribers

Subscribers to an unquoted SA are liable from the moment they sign the subscription certificate for all losses arising from a failure to execute their obligation to pay in capital to the other subscribers of the shares.

Subscribers are liable to third parties only for the amount they have contributed to share capital.

Ownership

Type of Shares

The minimum legal par value of a share is F 100. Shares must be nominative, not bearer, and may be issued for cash or in kind (in the latter case the contribution must be valued by an independent appraiser appointed by the Commercial Court and the valuation annexed to the articles). All shares must be issued at time of registration and one quarter of the par value of these shares must be paid in; the remaining 75 per cent is due at the call of the board of directors or directorate within five years from the date of registration.

There are three classes of shares: common, preferred and non-voting (the latter would have preferential rights to dividends and distributions in a liquidation and may not be issued to any member of management). Ownership of shares is evidenced by entries on the SA's share transfer register and by an account opened with the depositary or with an approved financial intermediary.

There must be at least seven shareholders in an SA. It is they who appoint the management, the auditor, declare dividends, approve the issuing of debentures and approve financial statements and who may decide to dissolve the SA. Their liability is limited to the par value of their shares.

Dividends are payable out of distributable profits and any special reserves created by the articles. They may be declared only after the shareholders have approved the annual financial statements. Interim dividends however may be declared from time to time by the board of directors or directorate.

Meetings and Voting Rights

There are three types of shareholders' meetings: ordinary, extraordinary and special. At least one ordinary general meeting must be held annually to approve the financial statements. Shareholders having a right to vote and representing 25 per cent of the share capital must be present at the meeting in order to form a quorum. In default of a quorum, another meeting will be held at which a quorum is not necessary. A simple majority of the votes cast is required for the approval of a measure and shareholders may give proxies to other shareholders or a spouse only.

Extraordinary general meetings must be held in order to amend the articles in any way, eg increase in capital, change of registered office etc. At least half the voting capital must be represented at the meeting in order to have a quorum. If a second call is necessary, 25 per cent of the voting share capital is necessary for a quorum. A 75 per cent majority is required for the approval of a measure. If a modification to the rights of a particular class of shares is proposed an extraordinary general meeting must be held as well as a special meeting of the class of shareholders concerned.

The number of votes per share is proportional to the percentage of share capital held, each share having at least one vote, and each shareholder is limited to a maximum of 10 votes. Limitations on the number of votes per shareholder may be imposed on all the members of a particular class.

Protection of Minority Owners

In order to prevent the usurpation of power by the majority shareholders, certain specific provisions have been enacted into French law.

One or several shareholders representing at least 10 per cent of the share capital have the right, within thirty days of the nomination of the statutory auditor, to bring an action before the president of the local Commercial Court to object to this nomination and petition for the nomination of an alternative auditor.

One or more shareholders representing 10 per cent of the share capital may demand the appointment of an expert to report on aspects of the management of the SA. This report must be attached to the company's financial statements and distributed to all shareholders.

Jurisprudence has recognised and developed the right of the minority shareholders to bring an action in order to have any act of the general meeting or the board of directors declared null and void if it can be proved that the act had as its real object the satisfaction of the personal interests of certain shareholders, as opposed to the protection of the SA's rights and interests.

Finally, minority shareholders may put written questions to the board of directors on any matter which concerns the running of the company. The response must be communicated to the statutory auditor.

Transfer of Ownership

Transfer of shares is evidenced by a transfer order (*ordre de mouvement*) prepared by the shareholder and accomplished when the transaction is recorded in the company's account. However, in the case of shares issued for in kind contributions, transfer is not permitted until after two years from date of registration and then must be evidenced by transfer deed. Shares are freely transferable to third parties unless the articles stipulate otherwise, but shares qualifying a director may not be transferred.

In general, the SA may not purchase its own shares. Exceptions to this rule do exist for certain special purposes, but any such purchase must be approved by the shareholders.

Dissolution/Winding Up

If an SA, due to financial difficulties, is unable to pay its creditors, the Commercial Court may be petitioned to take whatever action is necessary by a creditor, a shareholder or the State Prosecutor.

The Court may order a period of observation which may last up to two years. All normal business (except the mortgaging of assets) of the SA may continue during this period. A receiver, a creditor's representative and an employee representative will be appointed by the Court.

If after this period, the receiver decides that the financial difficulties cannot be solved, a bankruptcy (*liquidation des biens*) will be recommended. If the Court agrees with this decision, the SA will be wound up. If a solution is deemed possible a reconstruction plan must be submitted to the Court. If approved, this plan is then implemented under the supervision of parties appointed by the Court.

Dissolution of the SA will occur after the expiration of 99 years, destruction of the assets or achievement of purpose, if the number of shareholders falls below seven, the capital falls below F 250,000 or voluntarily at an extraordinary general meeting. A shareholder may also petition the Court for a dissolution. The fact must be published and filed with the clerk of the Commercial Court.

Liquidation (*dépôt de bilan*) occurs as a result of dissolution. The shareholders designate a liquidator who then assumes all managerial functions. This appointment and the eventual final liquidation must be published and notified to the Commercial Court.

Management

Management of an SA may be entrusted to either a board of directors (*conseil d'administration*) or a supervisory council (*conseil de surveillance*).

Board of Directors

Each member of the board must be a shareholder, the minimum number of shares required for this purpose being specified in the articles. These shares are inalienable and should be in nominative form. The first board is appointed in the articles and subsequent appointments are made at ordinary general meetings of the shareholders. The minimum legal membership is three (with a maximum of 12); if membership falls below this number, the remaining directors must call a shareholders' meeting to appoint a new board.

The maximum term of membership on the board is six years. Removal from the board may be made by a simple majority vote of the shareholders. Any change in the board must be published and notified to the various government authorities.

The board has full power to direct the affairs of the SA and decisions are made by a majority vote at a duly convened meeting at which half of the directors are present.

Executive Officers/Management

The principal officer is the Principal Director General (PDG) who is selected by the board from among its members. Maximum term of office is six years and removal at any stage is by the board. If the PDG is not a French citizen it may be necessary for him to obtain a Commercial Card. The PDG's major roles are to carry out the actual management of the corporation and to represent, act for and bind the corporation within the limitation of the objects of the company and the provisions of the Articles.

Other officers include general managers, whose role is to assist the PDG. These may, but need not, be directors and are appointed and removed by the board of directors.

Directorate and Supervisory Council
If an SA chooses this form of management, then it must be indicated on its letter head and all other communications with the public.

The council has a minimum of three and a maximum of 12 members. These may be French, foreign nationals or legal entities, and are appointed by (if not named originally in the articles) and removed by the shareholders (maximum term six years), and each member must be a shareholder. A certain number of members may also be elected by the employees. The main function of the council is to appoint and control the directorate.

The members of the directorate are appointed by the council, and may consist at most of five members. A one person directorate (*directeur général unique*) is possible where the capital is less than F 600,000. They must be individuals who are not members of the council, do not have to be shareholders and their maximum term of office is four years. The purpose of the directorate is to manage the SA and its powers are limited only by the corporate purpose and the articles. Any limitation on the directorate's powers is binding within the corporation but cannot be asserted against third parties.

The directorate must submit a quarterly operating report to the supervisory council. Dismissal of the members of the directorate is by proposal of the council as approved at an ordinary general meeting.

Statutory Auditors
The SA must have at least one statutory auditor, who is otherwise independent. His principal functions, mainly supervisory, are to certify the accuracy of the financial statements of the SA and financial data submitted to the shareholders. An alternate auditor must also be appointed in case of death or incapacity.

Formation Expenses and Taxation
Costs of Registering and Forming a Company
These costs are exactly the same as those for the formation of the SARL.

Capital Taxes
The same distinctions and tax rates apply as for a SARL.

Fundamental Legislative Texts

- Code Civil, art. 1832 through 1844-17;
- Law No 66-537 of 24 July 1966;
- Decree No 67-236 of 23 March 1967;
- Decree No 78-704 of 3 July 1978;
- Finance Act 1982 — 30 December 1981;
- Law No 83-1 of 3 January 1983;
- Decree No 83-359 of 2 May 1984;
- Decree No 84-406 of 30 May 1984;
- Order of 24 September 1984;
- Circular of 24 October 1985;
- Decree No 86-584 of 14 March 1986.

GERMANY

(FEDERAL REPUBLIC OF)

PRIVATE COMPANY
(Gesellschaft mit beschränkter Haftung)

PUBLIC COMPANY
(Aktiengesellschaft)

INTRODUCTION

There are few restrictions on foreign investment in Germany that do not also apply to German nationals. Foreign enterprises that provide employment opportunities within the Federal Republic are particularly welcome, and have the same rights and obligations as any German company. There are no regulations prohibiting foreign corporations from owning the total capital stock of a German company, nor are there any restrictions on the transfer of profits to foreign investors or on the repatriation of capital.

Exchange control regulations are laid down in the Foreign Trade Act/Foreign Trade Regulation (*Außenwirtschaftgesetz/- Verordnung*). Under this act the government is empowered to restrict foreign investment if this is considered necessary for the stability of the German economy. Currently there are no restrictions in force. However, a foreign investor is under a duty to report his activities to the Federal Bank (*Bundesbank*), the body authorised to supervise the implementation of exchange control measures, if more than 25 per cent of an existing company's capital is acquired or if a company or branch is formed, acquired, sold or liquidated, provided the investment exceeds DM 20,000.

German civil and commercial law recognises a variety of types of business. Apart from partnerships the most common companies with limited liability are the Limited Liability Companies (*Gesellschaft mit beschränkter Haftung*) and the Public Limited Companies (*Aktiengesellschaft*).

In order to manage and operate a large corporate enterprise with large-scale public participation it would be advisable to set up an *Aktiengesellschaft* (henceforth AG). Small- or middle-sized businesses however would find it difficult to make the administrative as well as financial outlay which the Public Limited Company Act requires. A smaller concern would be advised to form a *Gesellschaft mit beschränk-ter Haftung* (henceforth GmbH).

PRIVATE COMPANY

(Gesellschaft mit beschränkter Haftung)

Documents

Memorandum and Articles of Association

A GmbH is usually established by two or more shareholders, although it may even be formed by one shareholder as a one-man-company (*Einmanngesellschaft*). Shareholders may be individuals or legal entities and they may be German or foreign. The founding shareholders have to agree on the articles of association.

Mandatory provisions of the articles cover:

- name and domicile of the company;
- objects of business;
- amount of share capital;
- amount of subscription of each shareholder, in cash or kind;

Optional provisions of the articles cover:

- names of managing directors. Although this is not mandatory, names of directors must be given to the Trade Register before the company is registered;
- competence to call the general meeting;
- participation and quorum;
- provisions for sale, assignment (especially pledge) or transfer of shares or parts of shares;
- limitations on powers of attorney for company director(s);
- fixing the fiscal year;
- distribution of profits;
- withdrawal and compulsory exclusion of partners;
- arbitration clauses;
- provision for the increase of share capital.

Minute Book

Resolutions of shareholders' meetings must be in writing but they need not be notarised.

Shareholders' Register

Although there are no formal requirements to keep a register of the shareholders, the directors must each year in January file an updated list of shareholders with the Commercial Registry.

Accounting Books

Sections 238, 239 and 240 of the Commercial Code require a GmbH to keep necessary trade books, inventory and bookkeeping records. The managing director of a GmbH is under a legal obligation to keep the books in an orderly fashion.

Registration Form

There are no special registration forms. The information to be submitted must at least mention:

- a guarantee that at least the statutory minimum capital has been paid in;
- by whom it has been paid in;
- name and address of managing director;
- the signature of the managing director.

This document needs to be notarised. It must be accompanied by:

- the articles of incorporation and other documents relating to the formation;
- list of shareholders;
- document of appointment of managing director(s) (if not contained in the memorandum);
- if, because of the purpose of the GmbH, permission to operate is required, documentary evidence of such permission;
- if contributions are made in kind, the contract relating to the transaction, plus documents demonstrating the adequacy of the contribution.

Registration Requirements

Trade and Industry

The GmbH must be registered at the local Trade Register which will be kept at the local magistrates court (*Amtsgericht*).

Where the company is founded by a foreign parent the following documents must be presented:

- a certified copy of the certificate of incorporation;

- a certified power of attorney for the agent who acts on behalf of the parent company in the formation proceedings.

Under the Hague Convention of 1961 legalisation of such documents by a German Consul is no longer required. However, as regards the UK, such documents have to bear the 'Apostille' which may be obtained from the Foreign and Commonwealth Office in London.

Tax Authority

Notice has to be given to the tax authorities after the GmbH is registered. The tax authorities will then allocate a tax number to the company.

Other Authority

Membership of the local chambers of commerce is obligatory. The chambers will also help with any queries.

If the company is set up by business people from the EC the *Landeszentralbank*, the local branch of the Federal Bank (*Bundesbank*) must be notified under exchange control regulations.

Capital Requirements

Minimum Amount

The minimum capital of a GmbH is DM 50,000. It has to be expressed in German Marks and fully subscribed.

At the time the company is registered (being also the time the company is established) at least DM 25,000 have to be paid into the company's account. Also each shareholder has to have paid in at least a quarter of his subscription.

A distinct feature of the GmbH is that the registered capital cannot be reduced by open or hidden payment of dividends or the like. As long as the assets do not equal the registered capital, no capital may be repaid or lent, nor may dividends be paid thereon.

Type of Capital Paid In

Subscription can be made in cash or in kind. In the articles of association payments in kind must be fully described, and their values given in a special report.

The minimal nominal par value is DM 500.

Shares can be sold and transferred freely — in the articles it can be prescribed that all other shareholders have to agree to any transfer.

Shares in a GmbH are not traded on the stock exchange.

Limits to Liability

The GmbH is liable to third parties with all its assets. The shareholders are not personally liable to third parties except up to the amount of their subscriptions. Under certain circumstances the shareholders are liable to the company itself (eg for any outstanding payment in respect of the subscription signed by the shareholders).

Ownership

Type of Ownership

Although the articles may provide that share certificates may be issued, there is no legal requirement to do so. Even where certificates are issued, they cannot be negotiable instruments such as bearer certificates. Nor does the law require a company to keep a Stock Registry or other formal ownership record.

Voting Rights

Each share must have a par value of not less than DM500 and be evenly divisible by DM100. Shareholders have voting rights according to the amount of shares they own. Each shareholder has one vote for each DM 100 of a share value.

Protection of Minority Owners

Shareholders having at least 10 per cent of the authorised share capital can call a shareholders' meeting.

The managing director(s) have to present accounting and trading books and disclose further information about the company if so requested by a shareholder.

Transfer of Ownership

Ownership can be freely transferred by sale or assignment of shares. Such sale is subject to the formal requirements of a notarial deed. The articles can provide that each sale or assignment requires the consent of the majority (or other proportions) of shareholders.

Shareholders' Meetings

At the shareholders' meeting (*Gesellschafterversammlung*) the shareholders decide on company matters such as the conduct of the business, the appointment, supervision and removal of directors and the distribution of profits. The decisions taken by the shareholders are generally made by simple majority vote. A qualified majority of 75 per cent is required for amendments of the articles. Shareholders' meetings may be held by proxy, so that foreign companies or persons are not obliged to attend personally.

Dissolution/Winding Up

The duration of a GmbH is defined by the parties in the articles of incorporation.

Pursuant to s 60 Limited Liability Company Act, the GmbH ceases to exist in the following circumstances:

- on the date of dissolution as set out in the articles;
- through shareholders' resolution;
- from the date of commencement of bankruptcy proceedings;
- if a court finds the articles to be defective;
- the articles may contain further circumstances under which the company shall cease to exist;
- the shareholders may ask the court to dissolve the company if the company's objects cannot be reached.

Management

Board of Directors

A GmbH is managed by one or more managing directors (*Geschäftsführer*), who must be individuals but do not have to be shareholders of the company.

A managing director can be appointed by the shareholders either in the articles or by separate resolution. The managing director may be dismissed at any time by a majority vote of the shareholders.

If the director happens to be a foreign individual no work permit or residence permit is required. To a large extent the managing director can even perform his duties from abroad.

The managing director represents the company in and out of court. The power of the managing director can be limited by the articles or shareholders' majority resolution. Should the director nonetheless act *ultra vires* in dealings with third parties the company as a whole will be liable, whereas the director is only liable towards the company.

Supervisory Board

If a GmbH has a workforce of more than 500 employees the setting up of a supervisory board (*Aufsichtsrat*) is mandatory. At least one third of its members must be employee representatives.

Statutory Auditors

The managing directors are required to prepare an annual balance sheet (together with an annex explaining the figures and the methods applied in the balance sheet), a business report and a profit and loss statement. Both of these documents have to be submitted to the shareholders within three months (smaller enterprises within six months) after the end of the preceding financial year.

Unlike the AG, a GmbH is not required to prepare audited annual financial statements unless it meets certain requirements based on size and activity. For example, the annual financial statements of large or medium-size enterprises have to be audited. This applies to companies which meet more than one of the three following tests:

- assets exceed DM 3,900,000 assets (capital set out in the balance sheet);
- turnover exceeds DM 8,000,000 turnover in the preceding financial year;
- there are 50 employees or more by yearly average.

Formation Expenses and Taxation

Costs of Registering and Forming a Company

The notarial fees for registration of a GmbH depend on the amount of the original share capital. For a company with a share capital of DM 50,000, notarial fees will amount to about DM 500.

The amount due for registration stamps depends on the share capital. For a share capital of DM 50,000 approximately DM 100–200 will be due.

A registration tax of 1 per cent is levied on the share capital.

A GmbH can be bought off the shelf (*Vorratsgesellschaft*). The cost to buy a company off the shelf amounts to approximately DM 62,000, which includes the minimum capital of DM 50,000.

Company Taxation

The tax rate is 50 per cent on undistributed profits and is reduced to 36 per cent if profits are distributed to shareholders.

On dividends to be distributed to a German shareholder, a further 25 per cent withholding tax must be paid. However, the German shareholder can claim tax credit against his tax liability for the 25 per cent withholding tax as well as for the 36 per cent companies tax.

On foreign shareholders' dividends the GmbH is liable for a reduced withholding tax according to the provisions of the relevant tax treaties between the shareholders' country of residence and West Germany.

The GmbH is also liable for the municipal trade tax, the rate of which varies since each municipality has its own local rate. This tax is deductible from the corporate income tax.

Fundamental Legislative Texts

The most important regulations on limited liability companies are contained in the:

- Limited Liability Company Act;
- Commercial Code;
- Civil Code;
- The four EC directives on publicity (9/3/68), capital (13/12/76), amalgamation (9/10/78) and auditing (25/7/78), which have all been integrated into the first two acts mentioned above.

There are a great number of acts that may be relevant for limited liability companies. The most important are:

- Conversion Act;
- Several Co-determination Acts;
- Auditors Regulation.

PUBLIC COMPANY

(Aktiengesellschaft)

Documents

Memorandum and Articles of Association

There must be at least five founding members who may be either natural persons or legal entities and can be German or foreign. After registration the AG may become a one-man company. The founding members must between them subscribe to the whole of the company's share capital. The articles of an AG must contain:

- name of the company;
- domicile of the company;
- corporate purposes;
- amount of the share capital;
- the par value of the shares, number of shares of each par value, classes of shares;
- whether shares are bearer or registered;
- specifications of contributions in kind;
- number of members of the managing directors' board.

Furthermore the formation document has to state the founder members, the amount and type of shares taken by each founder member and the amount of capital paid in.

Optional provisions are possible but only to the extent they do not violate the law. Such provisions usually relate to the managing directors' board, the supervisory board and the stockholders' meetings.

Minute Book

Minute books must be kept for meetings of the managing directors' board, the supervisory board and the shareholders' meetings.

Accounting Books

Pursuant to ss 238, 239, 240 of the Commercial Code, every merchant, and therefore also a company, must keep standard bookkeeping, inventory and account books.

Company Announcements

Pursuant to s 25 Public Limited Company Act, the AG must make important announcements to the shareholders in the Federal Gazette (*Bundesanzeiger*) a state journal for such publications. Additionally announcements may be made in the company's journal.

Shareholders' Register

Pursuant to s 67 Public Limited Company Act, the AG must keep a register of shareholders and the number and amount of shares issued.

Registration Forms

There are no special registration forms. All founders and members of the board of directors and of the supervisory board shall apply to the court for entry of the AG into the trade register. The application may only be made after one quarter of the nominal value of each share has been paid in. Payments in kind have to be made in full. Evidence shall be submitted to that effect.

To the application there shall be attached:

- articles of incorporation;
- the records relating to the appointment of the board of directors and the supervisory board;
- the formation report;
- signatures of the members of the board of directors for deposit with the court.

Registration Requirements

Trade and Industry

The AG has to be registered at the local trade register which is kept at the local magistrates' court (*Amtsgericht*).

If a foreign parent is setting up a company in Germany the presentation of the same documents as for a GmbH is required.

Tax Authority

Notice has to be given to the tax authorities (*Finanzamt*) after the AG is registered. The tax authorities will then allocate a tax number to the company.

Other Authority

Membership of the local chamber of commerce is obligatory. The local chamber will help with any queries.

If the company is set up by business people from the EC the *Landeszentralbank*, the local branch of the Federal Bank (*Bundesbank*) must be notified under exchange control regulations.

Capital Requirements

Minimum Amount
The minimum legal capital is DM 100,000. Before registration at least one quarter of this amount has to be paid up.

The minimum share par value is DM 50.

Type of Capital Paid In
Contributions consisting of non-monetary assets must be specifically set out in the articles along with the party from whom the company is to acquire the assets, as well as the par value of the shares to be granted in exchange for the contribution.

Limits to Liability
The shareholders are not personally liable for the obligations of the company. However before registration persons acting for or in the name of the company are personally liable.

Persons participating in the formation of the company are liable to the company for the accuracy and completeness of representations made on formation. Founders, board members and formation auditors may be jointly and severally liable to the company.

The members of the management board are held to a standard of care exercised by a 'diligent and prudent business executive'. If this standard of care has been breached members are jointly and severally liable to the company for damages resulting therefrom.

Ownership

Type of Ownership
The shares of an AG can be in the form of bearer shares (*Inhaberaktien*) or registered shares, in the name of the subscribing shareholder (*Namensaktien*). Shares which are not fully paid when issued must be registered shares. Such shares are registered in the company's share registry with the name, place of residence and profession of the owner.

Voting Rights
Voting rights arise out of ownership of shares. Shareholders have voting rights according to the nominal amount of the shares they

own. Each share must have a par value of DM 50 or DM 100, or a multiple thereof. Thus, if a company issues shares of different par values, a share having a par value of DM 100, has twice the voting power of a DM 50 par value share.

The voting right may be exercised by the holder of a proxy. The proxy needs to be in writing.

Normally resolutions of shareholders' meetings are passed with a simple majority vote, unless the Public Limited Company Act or the articles require a greater majority. Each amendment of the articles requires a resolution of the shareholders' meeting. This resolution requires a majority of at least three-quarters of the share capital represented.

Protection of Minority Owners
A minority of shareholders may call a special meeting if they make up one-twentieth of the share capital.

Transfer of Ownership
Shares of an AG are negotiable securities which may be traded on a stock exchange. However, due to cumbersome listing requirements and procedure, only a small number of German AGs are actually listed on one of the eight stock exchanges. Shares are mostly sold and purchased through banks, with the certificates normally being left in bank custody. Exercise of voting rights by banks or other institutions by proxy is regulated in detail in the Public Limited Company Act.

Bearer shares are freely transferable by delivery of share certificates and without the need for registration. They are therefore more customary than registered shares. The transfer of registered shares is effected by endorsement. The articles of incorporation may make any transfer of registered shares subject to the prior consent of the company or board of directors.

Shareholders' Meeting
The powers of shareholders are set out in the Public Limited Company Act. Unless expressly stated to the contrary in the act itself, the regulations set out in this act are mandatory in all cases.

The shareholders exercise their power to control the company's policies in the shareholders' meetings, which must be convened by the directors.

Notice of the meeting must be published in the journal chosen by the company for this purpose. The meeting normally takes place at the registered office of the company.

Shareholders' meetings must be held at least once a year and must take place within the first eight months of the company's business year.

The shareholders' meeting must decide the following:

- appointment of members of the board of supervisors;
- allocation of profits;
- salaries of members of the boards of supervisors and managing directors;
- changes or amendments to the articles of incorporation;
- increases or decreases in the company's capital;
- appointment of inspectors to examine the procedure by which the company was incorporated;
- liquidation of the company.

An extraordinary meeting of shareholders can be called if necessary for the benefit of the firm in general. It is compulsory to call a shareholders' meeting if half or more of the share capital is lost in trading.

One important shareholder's right during meetings is the right to ask the managing directors to disclose information on all aspects of the company's business affairs.

Sections 118–147 Public Limited Company Act contain further details on shareholders' meetings.

Dissolution/Winding Up:

The duration of an AG is defined by the parties thereto in the articles of association.

Pursuant to s 262 PLC Act, the AG ceases to exist in the following circumstances:

- on the date of dissolution as set out in the articles;
- through shareholders' resolution;
- from the commencement of bankruptcy proceedings;
- if a court finds the articles to be defective.

Management

Board of Directors

The board of directors (*Vorstand*) is in charge of managing the company's affairs.

The board may consist of one or more persons. According to s 77 Public Limited Company Act, directors must act jointly but the articles can (and commonly do) provide otherwise and powers are granted to individual directors to act without a prior unanimous decision reached by the other directors.

The company will be held liable for any obligation entered into by the directors with third parties. This liability cannot be waived by any internal regulations of the company.

The board may set up its rules of business unless the articles already include such rules or unless the articles confer upon the supervisory board (*Aufsichtsrat*) the duty to lay out rules of business.

The board is appointed by the first supervisory board for a period of five years. If several persons are appointed the supervisory board may nominate a member as chairman of the board. The same person may not be a member of the board of directors and the board of supervisors; the functions are strictly separate and incompatible.

Board of Supervisors and Employee Participation

Each AG needs to have a board of supervisors (ss 30, 95–117 Public Limited Company Act). This board is the third important organ of an AG after the board of managing directors and the shareholders' meetings. The main function of the board of supervisors is to control the activities of the managing director or directors. This board also appoints the board of managing directors and reviews the incorporators' report. The board has to examine balance sheet, profit and loss accounts, the report of the company and the annual proposal on the application of profit. The supervisory board may determine that certain transactions which might significantly affect the company's financial position are subject to its approval.

The composition of the board depends largely on whether Co-Determination law applies (*Mitbestimmungsrecht*). Co-Determination law provides for the participation of labour representatives in the management of some, though not all, AGs by way of their right to be represented on the board of supervisors.

If an AG has a workforce of less than 500 employees the board of supervisors will consist of shareholders only. If an AG has a workforce of more than 500 but less than 2,000 the board of supervisors will consist of at least one third of employees.

If the AG has a workforce of more than 2,000 the board of supervisors will consist of at least one half employees. If the AG is working in the steel, iron and mining industries and has a workforce of more than 1,000 employees the board of supervisors will consist of one half shareholders and one half employees.

If the AG is a holding company in the steel, iron and mining industries the board of supervisors will consist of seven shareholders and seven employees plus one member elected by shareholders.

Statutory Auditors

A balance sheet and a business report have to be prepared by the board of directors three months after the end of the preceding financial year and be submitted to the board of supervisors for approval.

Balance sheets and business reports for medium-size and large-size companies (for definition see *Statutory Auditors* (GmbH) for limited liability companies) must be audited by an auditor who is appointed by the shareholders.

Auditors shall be chosen from chartered accountants for large companies. Medium and smaller companies may be audited by a sworn accountant.

Formation Expenses and Taxation

Costs of Registering and Forming a Company

The costs of establishing an AG with the minimum capital of DM 100,000 may be around DM 5,000 (including court fees for registration). This, however, varies to a great extent depending on the complexity of the matter.

AGs are not available for 'off-the-shelf' purchase because the formation procedure is too lengthy and complicated and the cost too high.

Company Taxation

The tax rate is 50 per cent on undistributed profits and is reduced to 36 per cent if profits are distributed to shareholders.

On dividends to be distributed to a German shareholder, a further 25 per cent withholding tax must be paid. However, the German shareholder can claim tax credit against his tax liability for the 25 per cent withholding tax as well as the 36 per cent companies tax.

On foreign shareholders' dividends the AG is liable for a reduced withholding tax according to the provisions of the relevant tax treaties between the shareholders' country of residence and West Germany.

The AG is also liable for municipal trade tax, the rate of which varies (between 12.5 per cent and 22.5 per cent of the business profit) since each municipality has its own local rate. This tax is deductible from the corporate income tax.

Fundamental Legislative Texts

The most important regulations on AGs are contained in the:

- Public Limited Company Act;
- Commercial Code;
- Civil Code;
- The four EC directives on publicity (9/3/68), capital 13/12/76), amalgamation (9/10/78) and auditing (25/7/78), which have all been integrated into the first two acts mentioned above.

There are a great number of statutes concerning public limited companies. The most important are:

- Conversion Act;
- Several Co-determination Acts;
- Auditors Regulation;
- Investment Trust Act.

GREECE

PRIVATE COMPANY
(Eteria Periorismensis Efthinis)

PUBLIC COMPANY
(Anonymos Eteria)

INTRODUCTION

This section examines two limited liability company types. The first type is the *Eteria Periorismensis Efthinis* (EPE), referred to as a private company. The second is the *Anonymos Eteria* (AE), referred to as a public company.

The incorporation requirements for both types of company are very similar, but the extent of government control for the AE is wider than for the EPE.

The main differences between the EPE and the AE are in the capital requirements and in the nature of the shares.

The minimum capital requirement for the EPE is Dr 200,000 and must be fully paid up at the time of incorporation. The capital is divided into quotas (shares) of equal value of a minimum of Dr 10,000 each.

The minimum capital requirement for the AE is Dr 5,000,000, to be fully paid up at the time of incorporation. The AE can issue bearer shares or registered shares, but for certain companies, such as banks and insurance companies, the shares have to be registered.

As far as exchange control is concerned, restrictions on certain capital movements to Greece from EC Member States have been removed in 1986, in order to comply with EC requirements of free movement of capital.

Foreign capital for direct investments, capital for the acquisition of real estate and for the acquisition of shares listed on the Athens Stock Exchange can be brought into Greece from any other EC Member State without restrictions.

PRIVATE COMPANY

(Eteria Periorismensis Efthinis)

Documents

Memorandum and Articles of Association
This document must contain as a minimum:

- type and official name of the company;
- exact indication of the aims and objectives;
- address of the registered offices;
- name, profession, residence and nationality of the founders;
- share capital;
- participating share and quotas of each quotaholder (hereafter referred to as shareholders);
- confirmation of paid in capital up to the required amount;
- description of any contribution in kind and their valuation;
- name of the shareholder making the contribution in kind;
- duration of the company.

Other agreements can be included but are not compulsory:

- additional contributions;
- prohibition of competition between the shareholders and the company;
- mechanics of share transfer and any restrictions thereon;
- provisions concerning the control of the administration of the company by the shareholders.

Minute Book
A minute book of the general meetings of shareholders and of the board meetings, if there is a board, must be kept.

Accounting Books
The EPE must keep the following books of account:

- balance sheet analysis book;
- general ledger;
- general journal;

- journal of year-end closing entries;
- subsidiary ledgers.

Registration Requirements

Court of First Instance

The company must be registered in a special book kept by the Clerk at the Court of first instance.

A copy of a summary of the articles of association must be filed for publication in the government gazette.

Tax Authority

The company has to register with the local tax authority in the area of the company's registered office.

Capital Requirements

Minimum Amount

The minimum authorised capital is Dr 200,000. The capital must be fully subscribed with a minimum of Dr 100,000 paid in.

Type of Capital Paid In

Subscriptions can be made in cash or in kind.

The value of contributions made in kind has to be assessed by a local committee set up for this purpose by the Ministry of Commerce.

Limits to Liability

Each shareholder's liability to third parties is limited to his contribution of capital.

Shareholders are liable to the company to pay in the amounts they have subscribed.

Ownership

Type of Ownership

Ownership is represented by quotas (for convenience hereafter referred to as shares; quotaholders are referred to as shareholders).

The share capital is divided into shares of equal value, not to be less than Dr 10,000 or a multiple thereof.

There must be at least two shareholders. The shareholders are neither required to be Greek citizens nor Greek residents.

No share certificates are issued, only quota certificates.

The shareholders are registered in a book which is kept by the Clerk at the Court of first instance.

A copy of the list of shareholders can be obtained by any member of the public, as can a copy of the record of all transfers of the shares.

Voting Rights and Meetings

All shareholders have a number of votes directly proportional to the number of shares they possess.

The general meeting of shareholders must be convened by the administrator at least once a year, within three months of termination of the prior fiscal year. If the administrator fails to do so, any of the shareholders can call a meeting.

Decisions at the general meeting are adopted with a dual majority (ie with a majority of the persons present as well as with a majority of the shares they represent).

The general meeting of shareholders is the supreme authority of the company and can decide on any matter.

Only the general meeting of shareholders is competent to decide on the following matters:

- amendments of the memorandum and articles of association;
- appointment or revocation of the administrators;
- redemptions from liability of the administrators;
- approval of the balance sheet;
- distribution of profits;
- decision to bring an action against any of the organs of the company;
- extension of the duration of the company;
- mergers;
- dissolution of the company;
- appointment or revocation of the liquidators.

A qualified majority (at least three-quarters of the shareholders present plus three-quarters of the share capital present) is required for any of the following decisions:

- amendments to the memorandum and articles of association, which must be made in the form of a notarial document;
- change of object of the company;
- increase of the share capital;

- decrease of the share capital;
- premature winding up of the company.

Unanimity is required for the following:

- change of nationality of the company;
- increase in the obligations of the shareholders;
- permission for the administrator to compete with the company.

Protection of Minority Owners
Shareholders representing one twentieth of the capital are entitled to call an extraordinary meeting.

Transfer of Ownership
Unless the memorandum and articles of association otherwise provide, there are no restrictions on the transfer of the shares.

The transfer of the shares can be made subject to certain conditions, such as the right of preference of the existing shareholders.

The company cannot acquire its own shares.

The memorandum and articles cannot restrict the transfer of the shares *mortis causa* or *dottis causa*, but it can be agreed that the other shareholders will buy out the shares inherited.

The transfer of the shares must be in a notarial document, published in the government gazette and registered in the register of shareholders.

Dissolution/Winding Up
A decision regarding the premature winding up of the company can only be made by the general meeting of shareholders with a special majority of three-quarters of the number of shareholders present and three-quarters of the share capital represented.

Only under certain circumstances can the court make a decision regarding premature winding up. The certain circumstances can for example be that the object and aims of the company are prohibited by law or that all the shares are in the hands of one person.

As soon as the share capital is reduced to one half of the original amount, the administrator must call a general meeting of the shareholders to decide on either an increase in capital or the winding up of the company. If the administrator does not call the general meeting or such a decision is not made by the general meeting, any person who has an interest in the company has the right to file a petition with the court and ask for the dissolution of the company.

Management

Board

The EPE is managed by one or more administrators, who can be individuals or legal entities. They need not be members of the EPE and neither have to be Greek citizens nor resident in Greece.

If no administrator is appointed, all founders are administrators and act jointly.

The administrator can either be appointed in the memorandum and articles of association or by decision of the shareholders at the general meeting.

There can be more than one administrator, who need not be a shareholder.

If the administrator is appointed in the memorandum and articles for a definite time period, he can only be dismissed for serious reasons by decision of the court, provided that a previous decision of dismissal was taken by the general meeting of the shareholders.

The administrator cannot compete with the company unless the general meeting of shareholders decided otherwise, by unanimity. He has full authority to bind the company in all respects, except in those matters reserved to the shareholders' meeting.

The administrator must prepare an annual inventory, annual accounts and a management report.

Statutory Auditors

There is no requirement for a statutory auditor for an EPE.

Formation Expenses and Taxation

Costs of Registering and Forming a Company

The expenditure involved in setting up an EPE includes the following:

- registration tax of 1 per cent of the share capital;
- notarial fees of Dr. 15,000;
- 1.3 per cent of the share capital for the Lawyers' Fund;

- Dr 15,000 for copies;
- Dr 30,000 for publication in the government Gazette.

Company Income Tax

The EPE is treated as a conduit for tax purposes. That is, taxable income which the company earns is divided among the shareholders according to their positions of the capital, and must be included in their individual annual tax returns.

Fundamental Legislative Texts

The EPE is basically governed by Law 3190 of 1955.

PUBLIC COMPANY

(Anonymos Eteria)

Documents

Memorandum and Articles of Association
The memorandum and articles of association must contain:

- type and official name of the company;
- precise indication of the aims and objectives;
- address of the registered offices;
- duration of the company;
- amount of the share capital and the manner of payment;
- number of shares of each class;
- provisions concerning the conversion of bearer shares to registered shares or from registered shares to bearer shares;
- rules governing the functioning of the general meeting of shareholders and quorum requirements;
- functioning and competence of the board of directors;
- control of the company;
- rights of the shareholders;
- distribution of profits;
- winding up and liquidation of the company;
- name and details of the persons who signed the memorandum and articles;
- the approximate cost of incorporation.

Minute Book
The AE must keep a minute book of the board meetings and a minute book of the general meetings of shareholders.

Accounting Books
The following books of account have to be maintained:

- balance sheet;
- general ledger;
- general journal;
- journal of year-end closing entries;

- subsidiary ledgers.

The balance sheet must be drawn up with absolute clarity and reflect the true financial position of the company.

Registration Requirements

Ministry of Commerce
The memorandum and articles of association must be approved by the Ministry of Commerce.

The Ministry's decision and the memorandum and articles of association must be published in the government gazette.

Prefecture
After approval has been granted by the Ministry of Commerce, the company must be registered with the local Prefecture of the district in which the company will be located. A file of the company is kept at the Prefecture.

Capital Requirements

Minimum Amount
The minimum capital of Dr 5,000,000 must be fully paid up at the time of incorporation, by at least two founders.

Where the capital exceeds Dr 5,000,000, at least a quarter of the nominal value of the shares in excess thereof must be paid up.

Where arrangement for partial payment of the share capital has been made, the period must be fixed in the memorandum and articles of association. The period cannot exceed ten years.

The amount of the share capital must be mentioned on any printed document issued by the company.

Type of Capital Paid In
Subscriptions may be made in cash or in kind. Where contributions are made in kind, the value of such assets has to be assessed by a local committee set up under the Ministry of Commerce.

The owner of a partially paid share which is transferred remains jointly and severally liable with the new owner for the balance during a maximum period of two years.

Limits to Liability
Shareholders are only liable to third parties to the extent of their contribution to the capital. Shareholders are liable to the company to pay in the amounts they have subscribed.

Ownership

Type of Ownership
The participants in the AE are shareholders.

There must be at least two shareholders, but there is no maximum limit to their number.

The shares can be bearer shares or registered shares. The shares of certain companies such as banks, insurance companies, railway companies and electricity boards must be registered shares.

Several classes of shares can be issued.

The nominal value of each share cannot be less than Dr100.

Voting Rights and Meetings
All voting shares have a right to vote at the general meeting of shareholders. The voting rights are in proportion to the quantum of share capital the share represents.

The general meeting of shareholders is the supreme authority of the company and is the only authority competent to make the following decisions:

- amendments of the memorandum and articles of association;
- election of the board of directors and of the auditors;
- approval of the balance sheet of the company;
- distribution of profits;
- debenture issues;
- mergers;
- appointment of liquidators.

The notice of convocation of the general meeting must be published and together with a copy of the agenda filed at the local Prefecture.

The ordinary general meeting is held at least once a year within six months of the end of the prior fiscal year.

Ten days before the general meeting, each shareholder is entitled to obtain a copy of the annual balance sheet, the reports of the meetings of the board of directors and the auditors' reports.

Shareholders of preferred stock with no voting rights may participate in the meeting but not vote.

If one-fifth of the paid up share capital entitled to vote is not present or represented, the meeting must be adjourned to a later date at which any number of shares present will form a quorum.

Decisions on all matters other than those requiring a special majority may be taken by a majority of the shares present or represented at the meeting.

When a special majority is required, a special quorum of two-thirds of the paid up share capital entitled to vote is required.

The following decisions require a special majority:

- change of the objects of the company;
- increase of the obligations of the shareholders;
- increase and decrease of the share capital;
- issuing of debentures;
- merger;
- extension of the duration;
- premature winding up;
- any other matter if so provided in the articles of association.

A special minute book of the general meeting of shareholders must be kept.

Protection of Minority Owners

On the request of shareholders representing one-twentieth of the share capital, the board of directors must convene an extraordinary general meeting of the shareholders within 30 days of such a petition.

Where the share capital of the company is at least Dr 10,000,000, shareholders representing one-twentieth of the share capital may request an auditing of the AE by filing such a request with the Court.

If the memorandum and articles of association so provide, minority shareholders representing up to one-tenth of the share capital may request that a decision on any issue on the agenda of the general meeting of shareholders shall be adopted by open ballot.

Transfer of Ownership

Registered shares are transferred upon recording the transfer in the shareholder register, which must be signed by both transferor and transferee. Upon the transfer a new share certificate is issued. The transfer of bearer shares is effected by the mere delivery of the share certificates.

Dissolution/Winding Up

As soon as the total assets of the company fall in value below a half of the original share capital, the board of directors must convene a general meeting of the shareholders to decide on dissolution or on a capital increase.

The company is dissolved upon expiration of the period fixed for its duration, in case of bankruptcy or after a decision of the general meeting of shareholders to that effect, adopted with a special majority.

The general meeting of shareholders appoints the liquidators. Until they are appointed, the board of directors act as liquidators.

Management

Board

The AE is managed by a board of directors consisting of at least three directors.

The initial board of directors is appointed in the memorandum and articles of association and is subsequently elected by the general meeting of shareholders. Their period of office cannot exceed six years, but they can be re-elected.

The board of directors meets at least once a month at the registered offices of the company.

The board is entitled to decide on any matter concerning the administration of the company and the management of its assets. Decisions are adopted by simple majority, but at least three directors must be present.

Acts of the board of directors which are beyond the objects of the company will bind the company against third parties, unless the third party knew that the acts were not within its objects.

Members of the board of directors have an obligation of confidentiality when information relating to the company has been communicated to the member in his capacity as director.

Statutory Auditors

The balance sheet and financial statements must be checked by at least two auditors appointed by the general meeting of shareholders.

Companies of a certain size have to appoint a special accountant, called a sworn-in-auditor, who must be a member of the official government body (SOL). A company that meets two of the following critera must appoint a sworn-in-auditor:

- balance sheet totals Dr 130, 000,000;
- annual turnover of Dr 260,000,000;
- annual average of 50 employees or more.

The sworn-in-auditors are entitled to convene an extraordinary general meeting of shareholders.

117

Formation Expenses and Taxation

Costs of Registering and Forming a Company
The expenditure involved in registering and forming a company includes:

- one per cent tax on share capital;
- Dr 55,000 for notary fees;
- Dr 50,000 for publication in government gazette.

Company Income Tax

Income Tax
An AE must pay the following annual taxes:

- 49 per cent on undistributed profits, which drops to 39 per cent in the case of companies registered on the Athens Stock Exchange, and 44 per cent on companies in certain industries, such as manufacturing and mining
- withholding taxes on dividends are also due on a scale ranging from 42 per cent to 53 per cent depending upon whether or not the shares are registered or bearer, and whether or not they are listed on the Athens Stock Exchange.

Capital Gains
Capital gains are taxed on income at the 49 per cent rate, although where the assets sold are intangible, the rate falls to 30 per cent. Gains from the transfers of immovable property, ships and shares in Greek corporations may be exempt.

Fundamental Legislative Texts

The AE is governed by Law 2190 of 1920, as amended.

IRELAND

(REPUBLIC OF)

PRIVATE COMPANY

PUBLIC COMPANY

INTRODUCTION

As in other jurisdictions, in the Republic of Ireland there are various forms of business structure available to the entrepreneur, ranging from the sole proprietorship to the public company with thousands of shareholders.

While the choice of form depends very much on the nature and size of the particular business, the two structures most likely to be useful to foreign businessmen are the private limited company and the public limited company, both of which are governed by the provisions of the Companies Act 1963, as amended by further Acts in 1977, 1982 and 1983.

In both types of company, shareholders' liability is limited to the amount of equity participation. The principal difference between the two vehicles is that the public company may be listed on the stock exchange, has a defined minimum capital, easier share transferability and requires a greater minimum but no maximum number of shareholders.

The vast majority of Irish companies, however, including the subsidiaries of foreign companies, are private limited companies.

PRIVATE COMPANY

Documents

Memorandum and Articles of Association

A memorandum of association is needed to incorporate a company, and must include:

- the name of the company, indicating that it is a limited company, either by using the abbreviation 'Ltd' or the Irish equivalent teoranta or 'teo';
- the objects;
- the authorised share capital and how it is to be divided into shares; and
- the fact that the liability of its members is limited.

For a standard form of memorandum, see ss 4(3),16, Sch 1 Table B, of the 1983 Act.

A company must also have articles of association or by-laws. If the founders do not specifically adopt an alternative set of articles , the model articles in Sch 1 Table A Pt II to the Companies Acts 1963 to 1983 will automatically be adopted.

Except for restrictions inherent in the general law, the Companies Act or the memorandum of association, there are no limitations on the contents of the articles.

The articles of association of private companies must, however, contain provisions:

- limiting the membership to 50 (apart from workers/ shareholders);
- restricting the transferability of the shares;
- forbidding the offering of shares or debentures to the public.

If any of these three requirements are not contained in the articles, the company will be considered a public company.

If the above three requirements are contained in the articles of association but are not complied with in practice, the company continues to be private but it loses the legal privileges of this status.

Offering shares or debentures of a private limited company to the public is a criminal offence and the company and its officers will be liable therefore.

There must at least be two subscribers to the memorandum, and the articles must be divided into paragraphs numbered consecutively and stamped.

The memorandum and articles of association must be printed and signed by each subscriber (founder), who in the memorandum must also state the number of shares taken.

The signatures must be witnessed, sworn and executed before either the solicitor dealing with the formation or one of the directors mentioned in Form 9b.

Minute Book

Minutes of the shareholders' general meetings are kept by the secretary.

Minutes of the proceedings of both board of directors and of their committees' meetings must be kept and signed by the chairman.

Accounting Books

Proper books of account must be kept by all registered companies, and should cover at least the following:

- income and expenditure (cash receipts and disbursements);
- sales and purchases (profit and loss account);
- assets and liabilities (balance sheet).

The profit and loss account and the balance sheet must give a true and fair view of the state of a company's affairs, and be submitted no later than 18 months after incorporation of the company and thereafter annually.

Before the annual meeting the directors are required to circulate their report on the state of the company's affairs to members and debenture-holders. The directors' report must suggest what amounts, if any, are to be paid in dividends and what amounts are to be retained as reserves. Furthermore, it must contain details concerning the company's subsidiaries and affiliates.

The auditor must in his annual report certify that the foregoing requirements have been fulfilled. A guideline to the contents of reports can be found in Sch 7 to the 1963 Act. A copy of this report must be annexed to the balance sheet before it is signed, and must be read at the annual general meeting.

Directors failing to take all reasonable steps to comply with the requirements may be fined up to a maximum of £500. If the failure to comply occurs within the two years preceding a company's winding up, directors may be subject to up to two years' imprisonment, a fine of up to £2,500, or both, for non-compliance.

Registration Form

There are a number of forms used for registration purposes which can be obtained from the Registrar of Companies. The memorandum and the articles of association must be registered with the Registrar of Companies, the files of which are kept at the Companies Registration Office.

Further documents which must be submitted for registration are:

- a statement of the names of the proposed first director or directors, first secretary or joint secretaries and the registered office (form 9b);
- a statutory declaration by a solicitor engaged in the formation, or by a person named as director or secretary of the company, of compliance with the requirements of the Act in relation to registration (form 41a);
- a statement of formation giving details of assets, liabilities, authorised capital, and of shares taken on registration for assessment of capital duty payable (form 25);
- a bankers' draft or cheque for the registration fee and capital duty.

Once the certificate of incorporation has been issued a private company may commence business and exercise borrowing powers.

Shareholders' Register

Every company must keep a register of its members at its registered office or at any other place the director(s) think fit. The register must state the names and addresses and number of shares held by each member and the date at which each person became (and ceased) to be a member. The register is to be open for inspection by members and the public during business hours.

Registration Requirements

Trade and Industry

Apart from registration with the Registrar of Companies no further registration is required, although certain types of businesses such as banking need special licences.

An Irish company issuing shares to non-residents will need exchange control permission from the Central Bank.

Tax Authority

Taxes are administered by the Office of the Revenue Commissioners, which operates through tax offices throughout the country.

Other Authority

Membership in local chambers of commerce is not obligatory.

It should be noted that various investment incentive schemes exist which may also be available for foreign investors. The relevant body for foreign investors is the Industrial Development Authority.

Capital Requirements

Minimum Amount

No minimum capital amount is required for a private limited company. Conditions for receiving a government grant, however, normally require that the shareholders' equity at least equals the amount of grant to be received. The equity can either take the form of share capital or of a subordinated loan.

Type of Capital Paid In

Subscribers must pay for shares in cash or kind.

Allotment of shares in return for service contracts or for contracts that can be performed more than five years after the date of share allotment is not allowed.

Apart from the above, payment may be made in kind. When payment is made in kind, the directors have a duty of good faith and honesty when determining the value of the contributions, and an independent valuation must be obtained.

Limits to Liability

Shareholder liability is limited to the sums which they have already contributed to the capital of the company, and to any amount still outstanding on their shares up to their par value and any premium on them.

Ownership

Type of Ownership

There must be at least two subscribers (founders), each taking one share in the company on formation.

There are no restrictions on the category of subscribers, thus anyone can subscribe, whether Irish or foreign.

Shares must have a nominal or par value.

Voting Rights

One vote attaches to every share or to each £10 stock unless the regulations provide otherwise. The right to vote may be exercised by written proxy. It can be provided in the memorandum and articles of association that special share categories only carry restricted voting rights or no vote at all.

Every company must hold an annual meeting and not more than 15 months may elapse between meetings. The principal business transacted at such meetings include consideration of the auditors' and board of directors' reports, electing directors, declaring dividends, and appointing auditors.

Extraordinary general meetings may be called to deal with specific problems.

The articles of association provide for notice procedures, quorums and voting majorities for resolutions. Certain types of decisions, such as removal of directors or auditors, may require extended notice periods.

The Companies Act provides certain minimal guidelines in some circumstances. For example, the quorum for a shareholders' meeting is two members present in person, unless the articles provide otherwise.

Protection of Minority Owners

Under s 205 of the Act the courts are given jurisdiction to remedy unprincipled conduct in the company even where no legal right has been infringed. A shareholder may start proceedings if:

- the affairs of the company are being conducted in an oppressive manner;
- the powers of the directors of the company are being exercised in an oppressive manner;
- the affairs of the company are being conducted in disregard of the interests of the shareholders;

- the powers of the directors are being exercised in disregard of the interests of the shareholders.

Unlike British courts, the Irish courts are not forced to find grounds justifying an equitable winding up of the company.

The court may make any conceivable order affecting the participants in the company. It may direct or prohibit any act or cancel or vary any transaction. The order may be for regulating the conduct of the company's affairs in the future or for the purchase of the shares of any member of the company by other members of the company or by the company or otherwise.

Transfer of Ownership

Shares can be transferred freely provided the memorandum and articles of association do not contain any restrictions as to transferability. In a transfer of shares the seller ceases to be a member of the company, and thus ceases to be liable for calls on the shares when the transfer was made in good faith and has been registered.

Private companies are required to impose some restrictions as to the transferability in order to keep the private company status.

The restrictions include a right of pre-emption whereby it is in the directors' absolute discretion to decline to register transfer of shares if the requirements have not been fulfilled.

Transfer of ownership to existing members cannot be refused.

Dissolution/Winding Up

Companies can be wound up in three major ways:

- by the members themselves in a voluntary winding up;
- by the creditors in a voluntary winding up;
- by the court in a compulsory winding up.

Statutory Instrument No 28 of 1966 contains the winding up rules for companies.

For a voluntary winding up, members must pass a special resolution that the company is to be wound up. The main difference from a creditors' voluntary winding up is that in the latter creditors instead of the shareholders have the right to nominate the liquidator and decide his remuneration. In both cases, three months after the Registrar of Companies receives the relevant documentation, ie the accounting of the winding up, the company is deemed dissolved.

Grounds for voluntary winding up are:

- shareholders may be dissatisfied with the way the company is run;

- shareholders may not be able to raise additional funds to stay in business;
- shareholders may realise that the company is becoming insolvent.

The most distinctive features of a compulsory winding up by a court are that:

- liquidation can be imposed on the company at the instigation of any member or creditor, or the Minister in special cases;
- the court appoints the liquidator and determines his fees;
- the liquidator is an officer of the court and works very much under its supervision.

Grounds for a compulsory winding up are:

- if a special shareholders' resolution approves the winding up;
- if the company has not commenced business within one year of incorporation;
- where membership falls below the statutory minimum;
- where the company is unable to pay its debts;
- where a winding up is just and equitable.

Management

The memorandum and articles of association provides the management structure for a company. By law, however, all companies are required to have at least two directors and one secretary, thus making it impossible to have a one-man company.

Every company must keep a registry of directors and secretaries with names, addresses, nationalities, occupations and particulars of any other directorships they may hold.

Board of Directors

If the model articles of association have been adopted, the board will possess considerable power to manage the business of the company, including power to call the annual general shareholders' meeting.

Provisions in the articles may, however, restrict the board's decision making, so that certain decisions must be taken by a resolution of all members or be subject to certain shareholders' decision or veto.

The directors determine the frequency and procedure of board meetings, insofar as they are not regulated by law. The law prescribes that any director at any time may summon a board meeting and that all directors must be given reasonable notice. The notice requirement need not be observed if the director is abroad and all the other board members agree.

The quorum requirement is two board members. The board's decisions are taken by majority vote in a meeting or by a written resolution signed by all entitled to receive notice of board meetings.

Employee Representation

Workers' participation at board level exists for semi-State enterprises. Such legislation does not apply to the private industry. Joint employer/union councils are a matter for negotiation between unions and management.

Executive Officers/Management

Every company must have a secretary. No particular qualifications are required for the post. Duties of a secretary include:

- making appropriate statutory declarations prerequisite to the commencement of business of a public company;
- signing annual returns and accompanying documents;
- verifying statements of affairs required by the court in a compulsory winding up;
- verifying statements of affairs submitted to a receiver;
- issuing share certificates;
- keeping company's registers.

Statutory Auditors

The Companies Act requires that the accounts which are to be presented to a company's annual general meeting first be audited. Persons undertaking company audits must be qualified accountants.

The auditor's duty is to examine the company's accounts for a financial year, which the director will lay before a general meeting, and to make a report on those accounts. It is the duty of the company's auditor to carry out such investigations as will enable him to form an opinion as to

- whether proper accounting records have been kept by the company; and
- whether the balance sheet is in agreement with the accounting records and returns.

Every auditor of a company has a right of access at all times to the company's books and accounts.

Formation Expenses and Taxation

Costs of Registering and Forming a Company
On registration of a company, a registration fee of £110 and a general duty and filing fee of £17.50 become payable.

Taxes on Registered Capital and Others
When shares are taken up by subscribers, a capital duty on shares of one per cent of the value of the shares becomes payable.

The corporate tax year is the calendar year. Alternative fiscal years are permitted.

The rate of corporation tax on income and capital gains is 50 per cent. However investment incentives may provide for a 10 per cent rate of corporation tax. Such incentives exist for instance for all companies which manufacture in Ireland, for companies in the Shannon area if they use Shannon Airport, and for certain services provided from the Dublin Customs House Docks Area.

Non-resident companies receiving interest or royalties are subject to a lower tax rate of 35 per cent provided they do not carry on a trade or business in Ireland. Also, the rate of capital gains tax payable by a non-resident on chargeable gains realised in respect of Irish assets varies between 30 to 60 per cent, depending on the period of ownership.

Resident companies must account for advance corporation tax (ACT) on distributions. ACT may be set off, within certain limits, against tax on income but not on chargeable gains. ACT is not payable on dividends paid by an Irish resident company to a 75 per cent parent company resident in a country with which Ireland has a tax treaty.

Closely held companies, that is, those which are under the control of five or fewer persons, are subject to the requirements that they must distribute income within a period of 18 months. Failure to distribute will result in an additional 20 per cent corporation tax charge.

Subject to tax treaties, double taxation relief is available for a company resident in Ireland with income or capital gains from any foreign sources. The Irish company is entitled to claim credit for foreign taxes paid against the tax payable in Ireland on the same income or gains.

Fundamental Legislative Texts

- Companies Act 1963;
- Companies (Amendment) Acts of 1977, 1982 and 1983;
- European Communities (Company) Regulation 1973;
- European Communities (Stock Exchange) Regulations 1984;
- Stock Transfer Act 1963;
- Companies (Forms) Orders 1964 to 1983;
- Companies (Fees) Orders 1964 to 1983;
- Companies (Reconstruction of Records) Act 1924.

PUBLIC COMPANY

Public Limited Company (Plc)

Documents

Memorandum and Articles of Association

As with private limited companies, a memorandum of association is necessary to incorporate a public limited company. It must contain the following:

- the name of the company, indicating that it is a public limited company by including PLC or the Irish equivalent;
- the objects of the company;
- the authorised share capital and how it is to be divided into shares.

A PLC can either be limited by shares or by guarantee. For standard models of a memorandum, see the second schedule of the 1983 Act.

If the founders do not specifically adopt any articles of association, the model articles set out in Sch 1 Table A of the 1963 Act can be adopted either in full or in part. For companies limited by guarantee further information is required.

As with private limited companies, except for restrictions in the general law, the Companies Acts, or the memorandum of association, there are no limits on the contents of the articles.

The articles of association of listed companies, however, must comply with stock exchange rules. These contain provisions as to the transfer of securities, share certificates, dividends, directors, accountants, rights, notices, redeemable shares, capital structure, voting entitlements and proxies.

There must at least be seven subscribers to the memorandum and the articles must be divided into paragraphs which must be numbered consecutively and stamped.

The memorandum and articles of association must be printed and signed by each subscriber (founder) who must in the memorandum also state the number of shares taken.

The signatures must be witnessed, sworn and executed before either the solicitor dealing with the formation or one of the directors mentioned in form 9b.

Minute Book

Minutes of the general meetings of shareholders are kept by the secretary.

Minutes of the proceedings of both board of directors and of their committees' meetings must be kept and signed by the chairman.

Accounting Books

Proper books of account must be kept by all registered companies.

The profit and loss account and the balance sheet must give a true and fair view of the state of a company's affairs, and must be submitted no later than 18 months after incorporation of the company and thereafter annually.

Before the annual meeting the directors are required to circulate their report on the state of the company's affairs to members and debenture-holders. The directors' report must recommend amounts to be paid in dividends and amounts to be retained as reserves. Furthermore, it must contain details concerning the company's subsidiaries and affiliates.

The auditor must in his annual report certify that the foregoing requirements have been fulfilled. A guideline to the contents of reports can be found in Sch 7 to the 1963 Act. A copy of this report must be annexed to the balance sheet before it is signed, and must be read at the annual general meeting.

Directors failing to take all reasonable steps to comply with the requirements may be fined up to a maximum of £500. If the failure to comply occurs within the two years preceding a company's winding up, the directors may be subject to up to two years' imprisonment, or a fine of maximum £2,500 or both, for non-compliance.

Registration Forms

The memorandum and articles must be registered the same way as above for private companies.

Public companies must also acquire a certificate to commence business from the Registrar before they can engage in any trading activity or borrow money. This is issued when the company has allotted shares to the nominal value of £30,000, paid up to at least one-quarter of that amount.

Shareholders' Register

Every company must keep a register of its members at its registered office or at any other place the director(s) think fit. The register must state the names, addresses and number of shares held by each member and the date at which each person became (and ceased to be) a member. The register is to be open for inspection by members and the public during business hours.

Registration Requirements

Trade and Industry
An Irish company issuing shares to non-residents will need exchange control permission from the Central Bank.

Tax Authority
Taxes are administered by the Office of the Revenue Commissioners, which operates through tax offices throughout the country.

Other Authority
Membership in local chambers of commerce is not obligatory. It should be noted that various investment incentive schemes exist which may also be available for foreign investors. The relevant body for foreign investors is the Industrial Development Authority.

Capital Requirements

Minimum Amount
The authorised minimum capital for a PLC is £30,000. Of the issued share capital at least one quarter must have been paid up.

Type of Capital Paid In
Subscribers must pay for shares in cash or kind.

Allotment of shares in return for service contracts or for contracts that can be performed more than five years after the date of share allotment is not allowed.

Apart from the above, payment may be made in kind.

When payment is made in kind, the directors have a duty to act honestly and in good faith where determining the value of the contributions in kind, and an independent valuation must be obtained.

Limits to Liability
The directors are personally liable for transactions entered into before the allotted share capital of minimum £30,000 has been paid up and before a trading certificate has been issued.

After formation the liability of the shareholders to third parties is limited to the amount of their share participation.

Ownership

Type of Ownership
There must be at least seven subscribers (founders), each taking one share in the company on formation.

There are no restrictions on the category of subscribers, thus anyone can subscribe, whether Irish or foreign.

Shares must have a fixed par or nominal value.

Voting Rights
One vote attaches to every share or to each £10 stock unless the regulations provide otherwise. The right to vote may be exercised by proxy.

It can be decided in the memorandum and articles of association that special share categories only carry restricted voting rights or no vote at all.

Every company must hold an annual general meeting and not more than fifteen months may elapse between meetings.

The principal business transacted at such meetings include consideration of the auditors' and board of directors' reports, electing directors, declaring dividends and appointing auditors.

Extraordinary general meetings may be called to deal with specific problems.

The articles of association provide for notice procedures, quorums and voting majorities for resolutions. Certain types of decisions, such as removal of directors or auditors, may require extended notice periods.

The Companies Acts provide certain numerical guidelines in some circumstances. For example, the quorum for a shareholders' meeting is three members present in person, unless the articles provide otherwise.

Protection of Minority Owners
Under s 205 of the Act the courts are given jurisdiction to remedy unprincipled conduct in the company even where no legal right has been infriged. A shareholder may start proceedings if:

- the affairs of the company are being conducted in an oppressive manner;

- the powers of the directors of the company are being exercised in an oppressive manner;
- the affairs of the company are being conducted in disregard of the interests of the shareholders;
- the powers of the directors are being exercised in disregard of the interests of the shareholders.

Unlike British courts, the Irish courts are not forced to find grounds justifying an equitable winding up of the company.

The court may make any conceivable order affecting the participants in the company. It may direct or prohibit any act or cancel or vary any transaction. The order may be for regulating the conduct of the company's affairs in the future, or for the purchase of the shares of any member of the company by other members of the company or by the company or otherwise.

Transfer of Ownership

It should be noted that although a non-resident does not need specific permission to acquire shares in an Irish public company quoted on the stock exchange, the transaction nonetheless must be handled either by an approved agent or an authorised depository.

Shares can be transferred freely provided the memorandum and articles of association do not contain any restrictions as to transferability. In a transfer of shares the seller ceases to be a member of the company, and thus ceases to be liable for calls on the shares when the transfer was made in good faith and has been registered.

Dissolution/Winding Up

Companies can be wound up in three major ways:

- by the members themselves in a voluntary winding up;
- by the creditors in a voluntary winding up;
- by the court in a compulsory winding up.

Statutory Instrument No 28 of 1966 contains the winding up rules for companies.

For a voluntary winding up, members must pass a special resolution that the company is to be wound up. The main difference from a creditors' voluntary winding up is that in the latter, creditors instead of shareholders have the right to nominate the liquidator and decide his remuneration. In both cases, three months after the Registrar of Companies receives the relevant documentation, ie the accounting of the winding up, the company is deemed dissolved.

Grounds for voluntary winding up are:

- shareholders may be dissatisfied with the way the company is run;
- shareholders may not be able to raise additional funds to stay in business;
- shareholders may realise that the company is becoming insolvent.

Grounds for a compulsory winding up are:

- if a special shareholders' resolution approves the winding up;
- if the company has not commenced business within one year of incorporation;
- where the membership falls below the statutory minimum;
- where the company is unable to pay its debts;
- where a winding up is just and equitable.

The most distinctive features of a compulsory winding up by a court are that:

- liquidation can be imposed on the company at the instigation of any member or creditor, or the Minister in special cases;
- the court appoints the liquidator and determines his fees;
- the liquidator is an officer of the court and works very much under its supervision.

Management

All companies are by law required to have directors and a secretary. The actual structure of the management is determined by the company's internal rules.

The memorandum and articles of association provides the management structure for a company. By law, however, all companies are required to have at least two directors and one secretary, thus making it impossible to have a one-man company.

Every company must keep a registry of directors and secretaries with names, addresses, nationalities, occupations and particulars of any other directorships they may hold.

Board of Directors

If the model articles of association have been adopted, the board will possess considerable power to manage the business of the company, including power to call the annual general shareholders' meeting.

Provisions in the articles may, however, restrict the board's decision making, so that certain decisions must be taken by a resolution of all members or be subject to certain shareholders' decision or veto.

The directors determine the frequency and procedure of board meetings, insofar as they are not regulated by law. The law prescribes that any director at any time may summon a board meeting and that all directors must be given reasonable notice. The notice requirement need not be observed if the director is abroad and all the other board members agree.

The quorum requirement is two board members. The board's decisions are taken by majority vote in a meeting or by a written resolution signed by all entitled to receive notice of board meetings.

Employee Representation

Workers' participation at board level exists for semi-State enterprises. Such legislation does not apply to the private industry. Joint employer/union councils are a matter for negotiation between unions and management.

Executive Officers/Management

A managing director can be appointed by the board and may be one of the board members. The board determines the term of service.

Management Committees

The board can delegate any power to a committee comprising at least one director.

Secretary

The status of the secretary is determined by the company's regulations. The secretary may be one of the directors but in cases where a decision can be made by a director and a secretary, the secretary/director cannot act alone.

Duties of a secretary include:

- making appropriate statutory declarations prerequisite to the commencement of business of a public company;
- signing annual returns and accompanying documents;
- verifying statements of affairs required by the court in a compulsory winding up;
- verifying statements of affairs submitted to a receiver;

- issuing share certificates;
- keeping company's registers.

Statutory Auditors

The Companies Act requires that the accounts which are to be presented to a company's annual general meeting first be audited. Persons undertaking company audits must be qualified accountants.

The auditor's duty is to examine the company's accounts for a financial year, which the director will lay before a general meeting, and to make a report on those accounts. It is the duty of the company's auditor to carry out such investigations as will enable him to form an opinion as to:

- whether proper accounting records have been kept by the company; and
- whether the balance sheet is in agreement with the accounting records and returns.

Every auditor of a company has a right of access at all times to the company's books and accounts.

Formation Expenses and Taxation

Costs of Registering and Forming a Company

On registration of a company a registration fee of £110 and a general duty and filing fee of £17.50 become payable.

Taxes on Registered Capital and Others

When shares are taken up by subscribers, a capital duty on shares of one per cent of the value of the shares becomes payable.

The corporate tax year is the calendar year. Alternative fiscal years are permitted.

The rate of corporation tax on income and capital gains is 50 per cent. However investment incentives may provide for a 10 per cent rate of corporation tax. Such incentives exist for instance for all companies which manufacture in Ireland, for companies in the Shannon area if they use Shannon Airport, and for certain services provided from the Dublin Customs House Docks Area.

Non-resident companies receiving interest or royalties are subject to a lower tax rate of 35 per cent provided they do not carry on a trade or business in Ireland. Also, the rate of capital gains tax payable by a non-resident on chargeable gains realised in respect of Irish assets varies between 30 to 60 per cent, depending on the period of ownership.

Resident companies must account for advance corporation tax (ACT) on distributions. ACT may be set off, within certain limits, against tax on income but not on chargeable gains. ACT is not payable on dividends paid by an Irish resident company to a 75 per cent parent company resident in a country with which Ireland has a tax treaty.

Closely held companies, that is, those which are under the control of five or fewer persons, are subject to the requirements that they must distribute income within a period of 18 months. Failure to distribute will result in an additional 20 per cent corporation tax charge.

Subject to tax treaties, double taxation relief is available for a company resident in Ireland with income or capital gains from any foreign sources. The Irish company is entitled to claim credit for foreign taxes paid against the tax payable in Ireland on the same income or gains.

Fundamental Legislative Texts

- Companies Act 1963;
- Companies (Amendment) Acts of 1977, 1982 and 1983;
- European Communities (Company) Regulation 1973;
- European Communities (Stock Exchange) Regulations 1984;
- Stock Transfer Act 1963;
- Companies (Forms) Orders 1964 to 1983;
- Companies (Fees) Orders 1964 to 1983;
- Companies (Reconstruction of Records) Act 1924.

ITALY

PRIVATE COMPANY
(Società a responsabilità limitata)

PUBLIC COMPANY
(Società per Azioni)

INTRODUCTION

This section deals with two company types. The first is the *Società a responsabilità limitata* (henceforth Srl), referred to as a Limited Liability Company. The second type is the *Società per Azioni* (henceforth SpA), referred to as a Joint Stock Company.

The Srl, and SpA are both limited companies.

In the Srl the participants are not shareholders as such, because no share certificates are issued. For ease of reference the participants will be referred to as shareholders.

Only shares in an SpA can be listed on the stock exchange.

In the SpA shares need not carry equal voting rights; provision for limited and different voting rights is contemplated in the Civil Code.

Recent foreign investment legislation may be of special interest to businesspeople contemplating company formation in Italy. Therefore, a brief summary is included.

PRIVATE COMPANY

(Società a responsabilità limitata)

Documents

Memorandum and Articles of Association

Two main documents are required for the formation of a company:

- *Atto Costitutivo*, analogous to the memorandum of association;
- *Statuto sociale*, analogous to the articles of association,

both of which must be deposited at the Register of Companies.

The *Atto Costitutivo* must be by public deed (Art 2475 of the Italian Civil Code) signed before a Notary Public and must indicate the following:

- the name, surname, address and citizenship of the founders/ promoters;
- the name of the company and address of the head office and secondary offices;
- the purpose of the company;
- the amount of issued and subscribed capital;
- the nominal amount conferred by every shareholder;
- the value of the assets and receivables conferred;
- the rules to be followed in distributing profits;
- the surname, name, place of birth and number of the directors and their powers, indicating particularly powers to represent the company;
- the number, surname, name, place and date of birth of the statutory auditors, who need be appointed only if the capital of the company exceeds It Lit 100,000,000 or if it is required by the *Atto Costitutivo*;
- the expected duration of the company.

The *Statuto*, or Company by-laws, contains rules concerning the inner workings of the Company, and forms an integral part of the *Atto Costitutivo*.

Accounting Books

The company must keep a daily record of transactions and an inventory book. These business records are to be kept in special books composed of consecutively numbered sheets, numbered before being used. Additionally, upon each such numbered sheet a notary or an official from the Companies Registry Office must affix his seal. The company must also preserve the originals of letters, telegrams and invoices for each transaction.

The company must draw up both a balance sheet and profit and loss statement in accordance with the regulations established by both the Italian Civil Code and tax legislation.

Minute and Other Books

The company must, in addition to the accounting books, maintain:

- a list of shareholders with an indication of their names and the payments contributed;
- a book containing a record of the proceedings and resolutions of shareholders' meetings;
- a book containing a record of the proceedings and resolutions of board of directors' meetings;
- a book containing a record of the proceedings and resolutions of statutory auditors' meetings (if this exists).

Registration Requirements

General Requirements

To form an Srl the capital must be completely subscribed and at least three-tenths of the cash contribution must be deposited with a bank.

The company name must include the indication 'Srl'.

The capital is represented by quotas of participation in the company.

Each quota must have a minimum value of It Lit 1,000 or multiples of It Lit 1,000.

Particular provisions for the formation of certain categories of company, depending on the purpose, may be established either by the government or by special legislation.

Registration with the Companies' Registry

Within 30 days after the *Atto Costitutivo* and *Statuto* are signed before the Notary Public, they must be deposited at the Companies Registry of the jurisdiction in which the company has its head office.

For contributions in kind, the sworn report of an expert designated by the President of the local civil court (containing a description of the property, the value assigned to each item and the standard of evaluation applied) must also be submitted. The court, after having ascertained compliance with the conditions established by the Italian Civil Code and after having consulted the Public Prosecutor, then orders the inscription of the company in the Companies Registry.

If the registration is denied an appeal can be presented within 30 days from notice of the denial.

The time required to form an Srl depends on the location of the court involved. The average time is between two and six weeks.

The *Atto Costitutivo* and *Statuto* must be published in the *Bollettino Ufficiale delle Società per Azioni e a Responsabilità Limitata* (BUSARL).

Once registered the company becomes a legal entity and receives a registration number, which must appear on company letterhead and other company correspondence.

VAT Authority
All persons and companies whose activity includes the delivery of goods or the supply of services mentioned in the VAT code are subject to registration with the local VAT administration (*Ufficio IVA*) as VAT taxable persons. The company thereby obtains its VAT Code Number.

Social Security Authority
Companies employing salaried individuals are obliged to register their employees with the National Institute for Social Security (*Istituto Nazionale per la Previdenza Sociale* (INPS)).

Capital Requirements

Minimum Amount
The minimum capital of It. Lit. 20,000,000 must be fully subscribed, but only three-tenths of the cash contribution need be actually paid up at the time of incorporation.

The capital is represented by quotas, each having a minimum par value of It Lit 1,000.

Type of Capital Paid In
Subscription can be made in cash or in kind. Payment in kind must be of property with an economic value.

If, after valuation, the real value of a contribution in kind is more than one-fifth less than the corresponding value of the capital, either the difference must be paid or the number of allotted shares reduced.

Limits to Liability

Shareholders are not personally liable for the obligations of the Company, except to the extent of the capital they have contributed.

Ownership

Type of Ownership

The participants in an Srl are quotaholders. For ease of reference, however, the participants will be referred to as shareholders, even though share certificates are not issued.

Shareholders

The company must be created by at least two shareholders, who may be individuals or legal entities.

If the *Atto Costitutivo* does not provide otherwise, the distribution of profits between shareholders is proportional to their respective quotas.

Voting Rights

Only shareholders who have paid up their quotas completely may vote.

Every shareholder has the right to at least one vote at meetings. If his quota is a multiple of It Lit 1,000, he is entitled to one vote for each It Lit 1,000.

Meetings

Meetings are convened by the directors and must take place at the head office of the company, unless otherwise provided in the *Statuto*.

Unless otherwise provided shareholders' meetings shall be convened by the directors by registered letter mailed at least eight days before the meeting to each shareholder at the address indicated in the list of shareholders.

The letter must indicate the day, the place, and the hour of the meeting, and an agenda of the business to be transacted.

Meetings are ordinary or extraordinary. Ordinary meetings should be convened at least once a year. The *Statuto* may provide for a longer time period, not exceeding six months, when particular reasons warrant.

The ordinary meeting:

- approves the balance sheet;
- appoints the board members, the statutory auditors and their chairman;
- determines the salaries of the board of directors and of the auditors, unless it is set out in the *Statuto*;
- decides matters pertaining to the management of the company that were entrusted by the *Atto Costitutivo* to the ordinary meeting or that have been submitted for consideration by the directors, or matters regarding the liability of directors and auditors.

An ordinary meeting also appoints liquidators and establishes their powers, as provided in Arts 2450 and 2452 of the Italian Civil Code.

For resolutions taken at a regular meeting to be valid and binding, they must be adopted by the majority of shareholders.

Shareholders can be represented by proxy.

Protection of Minority Owners

Meetings can also be convened upon the request of a minority of shareholders representing at least one-fifth of the Company's capital. The matters to be dealt with must be indicated in the request.

If the directors or the statutory auditors fail to convene a meeting, a meeting will be convened by Decree of the President of the local civil court, which appoints the person who shall preside over the meeting.

Transfer of Ownership

Quotas can be transferred either by contract or by testamentary (or intestate succession) provisions, unless otherwise provided in the *Atto Costitutivo*.

A transfer of quotas is valid from the date of its registration in the list of shareholders.

The transfer can be registered upon request of the transferor or the transferee, upon exhibition of the document evidencing the transfer, or else by declaration entered in the list of shareholders signed by the transferor and the transferee and countersigned by a director.

In the case of transfer of a quota, the transferor is jointly and severally liable with the transferee for payments still due on the quota for a period of three years from the date of the transfer.

SETTING UP A COMPANY IN EUROPE

Payment cannot be demanded from the transferor unless a previous demand for payment has been made from the defaulting member and refused.

Dissolution/Winding Up
An Srl can be dissolved upon:

- expiry of its term;
- attainment of the company's purpose, or the supervening impossibility of attaining it;
- impossibility of continuing operations or by the continued failure to hold shareholders' meetings;
- decrease of the capital below the legal minimum amount and where no provision is made for its increase;
- resolution of the shareholders' meeting;
- occurrence of other events contemplated in the *Atto Costitutivo*;
- Decree of the governmental authorities.

Following the decision to wind up the company, the directors cannot undertake new business transactions. If they do so they are fully responsible for operations undertaken.

The directors must convene, within 30 days of the event which requires dissolution, a meeting for approving dissolution.

The directors are responsible for the preservation of the company's assets until they are entrusted to the liquidators.

If company obligations are incurred during a period in which the quotas are shown to have belonged to one person only, that person is unlimitedly liable in the event of the insolvency of the company.

If the shareholders vote to wind up the company, their resolution must be published in the BUSARL.

Management

Board of Directors
The company is managed by one or more directors, who must be individuals. It is not necessary to be a shareholder of the company to become a director.

When management is entrusted to more than one person, these constitute the board of directors.

The appointment of directors takes place at a meeting convened for the purpose, except for the appointment of the first directors, who are designated by the *Atto Costitutivo*.

148

Directors cannot be appointed for a period exceeding three years.

A director who has the power to represent the company can perform all actions falling within the stated purpose of the company, subject to restrictions that may be contained in the *Atto Costitutivo* or his power of attorney.

Statutory Auditors

Statutory auditors must be appointed if the company's capital exceeds It Lit 100,000,000 or if the *Atto Costitutivo* so provides.

In companies without statutory auditors, every shareholder has the right to obtain information from the directors concerning the progress of the company's affairs and to inspect the company's books. Shareholders representing one-third or more of the capital have the right to have an audit performed of the operation yearly, at their own expense.

Formation Expenses and Taxation

Costs of Registering and Forming a Company

Annual tax on companies (*Concessione governativa*): It Lit 2,500,000.

Registration tax: one per cent of the company's capital.

Notary public's fees: It Lit 2,300,000

Yearly enrolment fees in the Chamber of Commerce: It Lit 306,000.

Corporate Income Tax

The company is liable for the following taxes:

- corporate income tax (IRPEG) at 36 per cent per annum;
- local income tax (ILOR) at 16.2 per cent per annum.

Shareholders are liable for a sliding scale personal income tax (IRPEF) on gross dividends.

Fundamental Legislative Texts

Italian Civil Code: provisions relating to *Società a Responsabilità limitata* are set out in Arts 2472 to 2497.

PUBLIC COMPANY

(Società per Azioni)

Documents

Memorandum and Articles of Association

The memorandum and articles of association must be by public deed (Art 2328 of the Italian Civil Code) and indicate the following:

- the name, surname, address and citizenship of the founders/ promoters and the number of shares subscribed by each;
- the name of the company and address of the head and secondary offices;
- the purpose of the company;
- the amount of issued and subscribed share capital and whether shares are registered or bearer;
- the nominal amount and the number of shares which constitute the capital;
- the rules to be followed in distributing profits;
- the number of board members and their powers, including powers to represent the company;
- the number of statutory auditors;
- the expected duration of the company.

The *Statuto*, or company by-laws, contain rules concerning the inner working of the company, and form an integral part of the *Atto Costitutivo*.

Accounting Books

The company must keep a daily record of transactions and an inventory book. These business records are to be kept in special books composed of consecutively numbered sheets, numbered before being used. Additionally, each numbered sheet must be sealed by a notary or an official from the Companies Registry.

The company must draw up both a balance sheet and a profit and loss statement in accordance with the regulations established by both the Italian Civil Code and tax legislation.

The company must also preserve the originals of letters, telegrams and invoices for each transaction.

Minute and Other Books

The company must, in addition to the accounting books, maintain:

- a list of shareholders (where shares are nominative);
- a book giving details of any debentures issued;
- a book containing a record of the proceedings and resolutions of shareholders' meetings;
- a book containing a record of the proceedings and resolutions of board of directors' meetings;
- a book containing a record of the proceedings and resolutions of board of statutory auditors' meetings;
- a book containing a record of the proceedings and resolutions of executive committee's meetings, if the company has such a committee;
- a book containing a record of the proceedings and resolutions of debenture holders' meetings, if debentures have been issued.

Registration Requirements

General Requirements

To form an SpA the capital must be completely subscribed, and at least three-tenths of the cash contribution deposited with a bank.

Particular provisions for the formation of certain categories of company, depending on the purpose, may be established either by the government or by special legislation.

The Company name must include the indication 'SpA'.

Registration with the Companies' Registry

Within 30 days after the *Atto Costitutivo* and *Statuto* are signed before the Notary Public, they must be deposited at the Companies Registry in the jurisdiction in which the company has its head office.

For contributions in kind, the sworn report of an expert designated by the President of the local civil court (containing a description of the property, the value assigned to each item and the standard of evaluation applied) must also be submitted.

The court, after having ascertained the observance of the conditions established by the Italian Civil Code and after having consulted the Public Prosecutor then orders the inscription in the the Companies Registry.

If the registration is denied, an appeal can be presented within 30 days from notice of the denial.

The time required to set up such a company depends on the location of the court. The average time is between two and six weeks.

The *Atto Costitutivo* and *Statuto* must be published in the special bulletin: *Bollettino Ufficiale delle Società per Azioni e a Responsabilità Limitata* (BUSARL).

Once registered the company becomes a legal entity and receives a registration number, which must appear on the company letterhead or other company correspondence.

VAT Authority

All persons and corporations whose activity includes the delivery of goods or the supply of services mentioned in the VAT code are subject to registration with the local VAT administration (*Ufficio IVA*) as VAT taxable persons. The Company thereby obtains its VAT Code Number.

Social Security Authority

Companies employing salaried individuals are obliged to register their employees with the National Institute for Social Security (*Istituto Nazionale per la Previdenza Sociale* (INPS)).

Capital Requirements

Minimum Amounts

The minimum capital is It. Lit. 200,000,000. The capital must be fully subscribed, but only three-tenths of the cash contribution need actually be paid up at the time of incorporation.

Type of Capital Paid In

Subscription can be made in cash or in kind. Payment in kind must be of property with an economic value.

If, after valuation, the real value of a contribution in kind is more than one-fifth less than the corresponding value of the capital, either the difference must be paid or the number of allotted shares reduced.

An SpA can also issue debentures for an amount not exceeding the paid in capital as substantiated by the most recent approved balance sheet.

However, this limited amount of debenture capital may be increased in special instances provided by law, as where the debentures are secured by an encumbrance upon real estate or by the Italian government.

Limits to Liability

Shareholders are not personally liable for the obligations of the company except to the extent of the capital they have contributed.

However, promoters are jointly and severally liable to third parties for obligations incurred before the company was registered. Registration of the company transfers responsibility to the company.

Ownership

Type of Ownership

The participants in an SpA are shareholders. Shares may be registered or bearer at the option of the shareholder, unless the *Statuto* provides they must be registered.

Shareholders

The company must be created by at least two shareholders, may be individuals or legal entities.

Pursuant to Art 2362 of the Italian Civil Code, when the capital is subsequently wholly owned by a sole shareholder, he will incur unlimited liability in the event of the insolvency of the company.

Voting Rights

Shares must be of equal value. They confer equal rights on their holders. However, a registered company's memorandum may divide its shares into different classes with different rights.

The following categories of shares can be issued:

- ordinary shares (*azioni ordinarie*) which confer ordinary rights;
- preference shares (*azioni privilegiate*), which give the holders priority in the payment of a dividend or in the reimbursement of capital, but confer voting rights for extraordinary meetings only;
- saving shares (*azioni di risparmio*) which can be issued only by companies listed on the stock exchange, and for a maximum amount of half their capital. They have no voting rights and offer higher interest than other categories of shares;
- enjoyment shares (*azioni di godimento*) which are given to holders of redeemed shares. Holders have no voting rights,

but participate in the distribution of profits remaining after payment to the unredeemed shares, for a dividend equal to legal interest on the sum invested. In the event of liquidation they participate in the distribution of the company's residual assets, after reimbursement of the other shares at par value;

- shares in favour of employees (*azioni a favore dei prestatori di lavoro*).

The value of shares possessing limited or no voting rights cannot exceed one-half of the company's capital.

Meetings

Meetings are called by the directors and must take place at the head office of the company, unless otherwise provided in the *Statuto*.

Notice of meetings must be published in the *Gazzetta Ufficiale della Repubblica Italiana* (Official Gazette of the Italian Republic) at least 15 days in advance.

This requirement is waived if the shareholders' meeting consists of persons representing all issued capital and all the directors and statutory auditors participate.

Meetings can be of two types, ordinary or extraordinary. Ordinary meetings should be called at least once a year, within four months from the end of the company's fiscal year.

The *Statuto* can provide for a longer time limit, not exceeding six months, when particular reasons so warrant.

The ordinary meeting:

- approves the balance sheet;
- appoints the directors, the statutory auditors and their chairman;
- determines the salaries of the board of directors and of the Auditors, unless set out in the *Statuto*;
- decides matters pertaining to the management of the company that were entrusted by the *Atto Costitutivo* to the members of the ordinary meeting or that have been submitted to its consideration by the directors, or matters regarding the liability of directors and auditors.

Extraordinary meetings may vote to modify the *Atto Costitutivo* and *Statuto*, and on the issue of debentures. Extraordinary meetings also nominate and determine the powers of the liquidators.

Both the ordinary and the extraordinary meetings can be held on either first or second call.

An ordinary meeting on first call is duly constituted with the presence of as many members as represent at least one-half of the company's capital, excluding shares with limited voting rights, are present.

An ordinary meeting on second call is convened when at an ordinary meeting on first call the proportion of capital required for a valid resolution was not present. On the second call, the meeting adopts resolutions validly no matter what proportion of the company's capital is represented.

An extraordinary meeting on first call adopts resolutions validly if votes representing more than one-half of the Company's capital are cast, unless a high majority is required by the *Atto Costitutivo*.

An extraordinary meeting on second call adopts resolutions validly if votes representing at least one-third of the capital are cast, except for resolutions concerning changes in the purpose of the company, its reorganisation, its premature dissolution, the transfer abroad of the head office of the company and the issuance of preferred shares. These decisions require the favourable vote of members representing more than half the company's capital.

A company with shares quoted on the stock exchange can convene an extraordinary meeting on third call if the above-mentioned proportions are not reached on second and third call. A resolution of such a meeting is valid and binding if votes representing at least one-fifth of the company's capital are cast.

Protection of Minority Owners
Meetings can also be convened upon the request of a minority of shareholders, representing at least one-fifth of the company's capital. The matters to be dealt with must be indicated in the request.

If the directors or the statutory auditors fail to convene a meeting, the meeting will be convened by Decree of the President of the local civil court, which appoints the person who shall preside over the meeting.

Transfer of Ownership
Bearer shares cannot be issued unless they are fully paid-up and are transferred by delivery.

The sale of registered shares may be subject to special conditions appearing in the *Statuto*.

Dissolution/Winding Up
A company is dissolved upon:

- expiry of its term;
- attainment of the company's purpose, or by the supervening impossibility of attaining it;
- impossibility of continuing operations or by the continued failure to hold shareholders' meetings;
- decrease of the capital below the legal minimum amount, and where no provision is made for its increase;
- resolution by the shareholders' meeting;
- occurrence of other events contemplated in the *Atto Costitutivo*;
- decree of the governmental authorities.

Following the decision to wind up the company, the directors cannot undertake new business transactions. If they do so they are fully responsible for operations undertaken.

The directors must convene, within 30 days of the event which requires dissolution, a meeting for approving dissolution.

The directors are responsible for the preservation of the company's assets until they are entrusted to the liquidators.

When shareholders vote to wind up the company, this resolution must be published in BUSARL.

Management

Board of Directors
The company is managed by one or more directors, who may be shareholders. They are appointed for three year terms and can be reappointed.

When management is entrusted to more than one person, these constitute the board of directors.

The appointment of directors takes place at a meeting convened for the purpose, except for selection of the first directors who are appointed by the *Atto Costitutivo*.

Directors cannot be appointed for a period exceeding three years.

A director who has the power to represent the company can perform all actions falling within the stated purpose of the company, subject to restrictions that may be contained in the *Atto Costitutivo* or his power of attorney.

Statutory Auditors
Statutory auditors must be appointed for three year terms and can be reappointed.

Pursuant to Art 2397 of the Italian Civil Code, the Committee of Statutory Auditors consists of three or five standing members, as well as two substitute members.

SpAs having a capital of not less than It Lit 500,000,000 select at least one of the standing members of the committee from the Register of Chartered Accountants, if they are three in number. At least two members must be chartered accountants if there are five statutory auditors. In both instances one of the substitute members must be chosen from the Register of Chartered Accountants.

Other SpAs select at least one of the statutory auditors and one of the substitute statutory auditors from the Register of Substitute Chartered Accountants.

Formation Expenses and Taxation

Costs of Registering and Forming a Company
Annual tax on companies (*Concessione governativa*):

- It Lit 200,000,000 — 499,000,000 capital: It Lit 9,000,000;
- It Lit 500,000,000 — 999,000,000 capital: It Lit 18,000,000;
- It Lit 1,000,000,000 — 4,999,000,000 capital: It Lit 30,000,000;
- It Lit 5,000,000,000 — 9,999,000,000 capital: It Lit 60,000,000;
- It Lit 10,000,000,000 upwards: It Lit 120,000,000.

Registration tax: one per cent of the company's capital.
Notary Public's fees: It Lit 3,000,000.
Yearly enrolment fee in the Chamber of Commerce: It Lit 306,000.

Corporate Income Tax
The following taxes are due:

- corporate income tax (IRPEG) at36 per cent per annum;
- Local Income Tax (ILOR) at 16.2 per cent per annum.

Shareholders are liable for a sliding scale Personal Income Tax (IRPEF) on gross dividends.

Fundamental Legislative Texts

Italian Civil Code: provisions relating to *Società per Azioni* are set out in Arts 2325 to 2461.

Further provisions are supplied by other statutes:

- DPR No 1127 of 29/12/1969;
- Law No 216 of 7/6/1974;
- DPR Nos 137, 138 of 31/3/1975;
- Law No 904 of 16/12/1977.

EC Directives on the subject:

- Dir No 68/151 of 9 March 1968;
- Dir No 76/91 of 13 December 1976;
- Dir No 78/885 of 9 October 1978.

Law (216/1974) created a system of public control, through an institution named Consob , for companies whose shares are listed in the stock exchange.

APPENDIX

Foreign Investment

(DPR 29/09/87 n.454, D.01/02/88 n.21)
From 1 October 1988, new laws allow the virtually free circulation of capital in and out of Italy.

An Italian resident can now undertake a whole series of transactions free from the constraints of and authorisations required by complicated Exchange Control Regulations, including the purchase of properties abroad, participating in off shore holding companies, entering into insurance contracts abroad, borrowing from foreign banks and credit institutions, purchasing foreign shares, and giving guarantees, avals, letters of comfort, bank undertakings, and performance bonds. All remaining restrictions on the free circulation of capital are expected to be removed by 1990.

Continuing restrictions include:

- no foreign bank accounts (unless in relation to the activities carried out by a local permanent establishment or in relation to the established foreign business activities of an individual);
- no purchase of bonds or securities maturing at less than 180 days;
- no fixed term foreign currency purchases;
- no sales and purchases between residents in foreign currency.

The State has preserved its currency exchange monopoly and consequently Italian residents are still required to convert foreign currency in their possession (in excess of approximately £1,000) within 60 days. All foreign exchange transactions will continue to be done exclusively through banking channels.

The position of the Italian importer (of interest to the foreign exporter) has improved. For transactions involving a value of less than approximately £4,000, a verbal communication to the bank will be sufficient. It will, however, continue to be necessary to fill in the forms for statistical purposes. For transactions over £4,000 it will be necessary to lodge a currency declaration. For certain transactions between £40,000 and £800,000 full documentation will need to be lodged with the bank, while all transactions over £800,000 will have to be fully documented.

One important effect of the new laws is that a UK company setting up a subsidiary in Italy will be able to retrieve profits and dividends and the proceeds of any sale of the business or assets without restrictions.

Obvious benefits present themselves to insurance companies wishing to underwrite policies for Italian residents and for lending institutions which want to do business directly with Italian companies or individuals. In this connection, obtaining security over locally situated assets will not present exchange control problems in the event of foreclosure and repatriation.

LUXEMBOURG

PRIVATE COMPANY
(Société à Responsabilité Limitée)

PUBLIC COMPANY
(Société Anonyme)

INTRODUCTION

This document deals with two types of company. The first type is the *Société à Responsabilité Limitée* (SARL), referred to as a private company. The second type is the *Société Anonyme* (SA), referred to as a public company.

Both the SARL and the SA are limited companies.

Both types of company are governed by the same fundamental legal texts, the major differences being the size of the capital and the nature of the shares.

Only shares in an SA can be listed on the stock exchange.

For manufacturing and trading activities, as well as for practising certain professions, a permit from the Ministry of Middle Classes is required.

Banking and insurance activities require authorisation from the Ministry of Finance.

In 1921 a Convention of Economic Union was concluded between Luxembourg and Belgium (BLEU). The two countries form a single Customs area free from internal tariff barriers and the Luxembourg and Belgian Franc are at parity with each other. There is only one foreign exchange control board for Luxembourg and Belgium, the *Institut Belgo-Luxembourgeois du Change* (IBLC).

In practice there are no exchange control restrictions. There are no registration requirements for foreign capital, so capital and earnings can be freely repatriated. The IBLC's main task is to ensure that the rules relating to the dual exchange markets (official market and free market), established to maintain the stability of the Belgian and Luxembourg Franc, are observed.

The system of dual exchange markets in Belgium and Luxembourg will have to be abolished by 1992.

162

PRIVATE COMPANY

(Société à Responsabilité Limitée)

Documents

Memorandum and Articles of Association
To form a SARL, at least two founders must appear before a notary and execute the *Acte de Constitution*, which must contain as a minimum:

- identity of the natural or legal persons who sign the *Acte de Constitution*;
- type and official name of the company;
- registered office of the company;
- object of the company;
- amount of the subscribed capital and, where applicable, the authorised capital;
- details of the different classes of shares, the rights attached to these shares, and the number of shares subscribed;
- whether shares are bearer or registered;
- details of contributions other than in cash, name of the investor and report of the auditor;
- nature of any privileges granted to the founders and reasons for granting the said privileges;
- where applicable, voting rights not representing stated capital;
- rules governing number and election procedure of the members of the board of directors, management and auditors, insofar as they are not provided by law;
- duration of the company;
- approximate cost of incorporation.

The *Acte de Constitution* must be published in the Official Gazette (*Mémorial*).

Minute Book
A minute book of the board of directors' meetings and a minute book of the shareholders' meeting must be kept.

Accounting Books

A SARL must keep books of account and certain records in accordance with accounting, tax and social security regulations.

These include the following:

- a journal for the entry of the day-to-day transactions;
- balance sheet;
- profit and loss account;
- a register of incoming and outgoing invoices.

Annual accounts must be filed with the Commercial Court and notice of this must be published in the Official Gazette.

Registration Requirements

Commercial Court

In each district a trade and companies register (*registre de commerce et des sociétés*) is kept at the Commercial Court, in which such information as required by law must be published. The register is open for public inspection.

A new SARL must register and provide the following information:

- type and object of the company;
- exact address of the registered offices;
- the share capital;
- names of the shareholders;
- names of the persons who are entitled to represent the company.

The name of the Commercial Court of registration as well as the registration number must appear on all deeds, notices, publications, letterheads, invoices and other documents issued by the company.

VAT Office

Where the company carries out a business activity, it is required to register with the local VAT office within 15 days of commencing such activity.

Capital Requirements

Minimum Amount

The minimum capital of LF 100,000 must be fully subscribed and paid up at the time of incorporation.

Type of Capital Paid In

Subscriptions can be made in cash or in kind. In the case of contributions in kind, an auditor must prepare a report describing the contribution and the method of valuation applied.

Shares issued in consideration for contributions other than cash must be fully paid up within five years after incorporation.

Limits to Liability

Each shareholder's liability is limited to his contribution to the capital.

Ownership

Type of Ownership

Ownership is represented by *parts sociales* (for convenience hereafter referred to as shares).

The capital is divided into shares of an equal value of LF 500 or a multiple thereof, and they must be fully paid up.

The shares must be issued to a named party and recorded in the shareholders' register. There are, however, no share certificates.

A SARL must have at least two shareholders (*associés*) and not more than forty. Shares in SARLs may not be offered for public subscription.

Voting Rights and Shareholders' Meeting

Each shareholder has a number of votes equal to the number of shares he holds.

An annual general meeting of shareholders is mandatory only where the company has more than 25 shareholders.

Where the company has 25 shareholders or less, shareholders will receive a copy of the proposed resolution or decision and may vote in writing.

Resolutions can only be adopted by a majority of shareholders representing more than half of the capital. If this quorum is not obtained at the first meeting or by written consultation, a second call will be made and resolutions may be adopted by simple majority, regardless the amount of capital represented.

Amendments to the articles and memorandum of incorporation require a majority of shareholders representing three quarters of the share capital. A resolution to change the nationality of the company can only be adopted by the unanimous vote of all the shareholders.

Protection of Minority Owners

Where the SARL has more than 25 shareholders, shareholders representing more than half of the share capital may request that a general meeting be convened.

Transfer of Ownership

Conditions for transfer of shares to outside parties are prescribed by law. The consent of shareholders representing at least three quarters of the share capital is required for any transfer, which must be effected by notarial deed and recorded in the share register.

Dissolution/Winding Up

The company can be dissolved by the court for special reasons.

Except for dissolutions by the court, the company can only be dissolved by a decision taken by majority of shareholders representing three-quarters of the share capital.

Management

Board of Directors

A SARL is managed by one or more managers (*gérants*), who must be individuals but need not be shareholders of the SARL.

The manager is appointed in the Acte or in a subsequent deed for a limited or unlimited period of time. Unless otherwise provided in the Acte, the manager can only be dismissed for valid legal reasons and has full powers to act on behalf of the company except for those matters which are reserved exclusively to the shareholders.

The company is bound by the acts of the manager, even if those acts are not within the objects of the company, except where it can be proven that the third party knew that the act was outside the objects. Knowledge cannot be imputed simply because the Acte was available for public inspection.

The manager must prepare an annual inventory, a balance sheet and a profit and loss statement. These documents must be submitted to the shareholders for approval.

Employee Representation

Companies with 15 employees or more must have employee delegates (*délégations du personnel*). The delegates must hold at least six meetings a year, including at least three meetings with the management of the company.

Their main task is to communicate with management and to safeguard and defend employee interests regarding working conditions, safety at work and certain benefits.

Employee delegates can only be dismissed in very exceptional circumstances.

A company employing 150 employees or more, must have a joint works council (*comité mixte*) composed by an equal number of employers' representatives and employees' representatives.

Statutory Auditors

A large and medium-sized SARL has to be audited by an independent auditor (*réviseur des entreprises*). A small company is audited by a statutory auditor (*commissaire aux comptes*).

A company qualifies as a small or medium-sized company where it meets two of the following criteria:

- annual turnover of less than LF 160,000,000 for small companies, and of LF 640,000,000 for medium-sized companies;
- total balance sheet of less than LF 77,000,000 for small companies and LF 310,000,000 for medium-sized companies;
- has no more than 50 employees for small companies and 250 employees for medium-sized companies.

The auditor is appointed in the articles of incorporation. Where there is more than one auditor they form a 'collège'. They cannot be appointed for a period longer than six years, but can be re-elected by the shareholders.

Formation Expenses and Taxation

Costs of Registering and Forming a Company

The expenditure involved, which is tax deductible, includes the following:

- registration tax of one per cent of the subscribed capital;
- notarial fees, calculated as a proportion of the share capital;
- registration with the *Registre aux Firmes* (LF 2,400 where the capital is LF 1,000,000 or less, LF 4,800 where the capital is more than LF 1,000,000);
- cost of publication in the Official Gazette, registration of proxies, copies etc (between LF 14,000 and LF 74,000).

Company Taxation

General Information

The corporate income tax rate is fixed at 36 per cent for both resident and non-resident companies. A further surcharge of 2 per cent is payable for unemployment contribution tax.

The corporate income tax applies both to the world-wide income of resident companies and to the Luxembourg source income of non-resident companies.

Apart from the corporate income tax payable to the state, a municipal business tax, fixed at approximately 9.09 per cent of the taxable income, is levied on behalf of the communes; it is deductible for corporate income tax.

The corporate income tax is levied on the corporation. It is also levied on the distribution to the shareholders except where investment of 25 per cent fulfils certain conditions.

The tax year is the calendar year unless otherwise approved by the Inland Revenue.

Taxable Events

Capital gains are taxable as ordinary income. Exempted are gains on sale of buildings or nondepreciable assets such as land that has been held for more than five years, provided reinvestment of the proceeds is made within two years in other fixed assets for use in the business in Luxembourg. The same exemption applies to gains on the sale of investments held for a minimum of five years. A restriction is imposed in relation to reinvesting the proceeds in shares of another company, in that the Minister of Finance must agree to both the sale and reinvestment in shares.

Tax may be deferred by reinvestment of gains from certain fixed assets if the reinvestment is made in business assets and within the following two years.

Also exempt are dividends from Luxembourg shareholdings of at least 10 per cent if held for twelve months preceding the year in which the dividends were received.

Losses cannot be carried back but may be carried forward for five years by residents and also by non-residents if so provided by tax treaties.

A straight-line method of depreciation is applied in the case of buildings (1.5 to 5 per cent), office equipment (10 per cent) and machinery (20 per cent).

A declining balance method for up to 20 per cent is available except for intangible assets and buildings.

Tax Incentives

For the first eight years of corporation, 25 per cent of the taxable income may be exempted from tax.

Investment credits are available and may be deducted from corporate income tax. These are restricted to new tangible assets not including buildings and motor vehicles.

Further supplementary investments may be deducted by 12 per cent from corporate income tax, provided the assets have a minimum life of four years.

Investment credit tax can be carried forward for four years.

Fundamental Legislative Texts

- *Loi du 10 Août 1915 concernant les sociétés commerciales* (as subsequently amended);
- *Loi du 23 Décembre 1909 portant création d'un registre de commerce et des sociétés* (as subsequently amended);
- Commercial Code Arts 8 to 17 and Art 189;
- *Loi du 28 Juin 1984 portant organisation de la profession de réviseur d'entreprises;*
- *Loi du 6 Mai 1974 instituant des comités mixtes dans les entreprises du secteur privé*, amended by *Loi du 18 Mai 1979;*
- *Loi du 18 Mai 1979 portant réforme des délégations du personnel*, amended by *Loi du 3 Avril 1980.*

PUBLIC COMPANY

(Société Anonyme)

Documents

Memorandum and Articles of Association (Acte de Constitution)
An SA must have a minimum of two founders who must execute the *Acte de Constitution* before a notary. The *Acte* must contain as a minimum:

- identity of the natural or legal persons who sign the *Acte de Constitution*;
- type and official name of the company;
- registered office of the company;
- object of the company;
- amount of the subscribed capital and, where applicable, the authorised capital;
- details of the different classes of shares, the rights attached to these shares, and the number of shares subscribed;
- whether shares are bearer or registered;
- details of contributions other than in cash, name of the investor and report of the auditor;
- nature of any privileges granted to the founders and reasons for granting the privileges;
- where applicable, voting rights not representing stated capital;
- rules governing number and election procedure of the members of the board of directors, management and auditors, insofar as they are not provided by law;
- duration of the company;
- approximate cost of incorporation.

Minute Book
A minute book of the board of directors' meetings and a minute book of the shareholders' meetings must be kept by the SA.

Accounting Books
An SA must keep books of account and certain records in accordance with accounting, tax and social security regulations.

These include the following:

- a journal for the entry of the day to day transactions;
- balance sheet;
- profit and loss account;
- a register of incoming and outgoing invoices.

Annual accounts must be filed with the Commercial Court and notice of this must be published in the Official Gazette.

Registration Requirements

Commercial Court
In each district a trade and companies register (*registre de commerce et des sociétés*) is kept at the Commercial Court, in which such information as required by law must be published. The register is open for public inspection.

A new SA must register and provide the following information:

- type and object of the company;
- exact address of the registered offices;
- the share capital;
- names of the shareholders;
- names of the persons who are entitled to represent the company.

The name of the Commercial Court of registration as well as the registration number must appear on all deeds, notices, publications, letterheads, invoices and other documents issued by the company.

VAT Office
Where the company carries out a business activity, it is required to register with the local VAT office within 15 days of commencing such activity.

Capital Requirements

Minimum Amounts
The SA must have a minimum share capital of at least LF 1,250,000. The capital must be fully subscribed and shares have to be paid up to the extent of at least 25 per cent.

The capital is divided into shares with or without nominal value. The nominal value cannot be lower than LF 50.

Type of Capital Paid In

Subscriptions can be made in cash or in kind. In the case of contributions in kind, an auditor must prepare a report describing the contribution and the method of valuation applied.

Shares issued in consideration for contributions other than in cash must be fully paid up within five years after incorporation.

Limits to Liability

Shareholders are only liable to the extent of their contribution to the capital.

Ownership

Type of Ownership

The participants in an SA are shareholders, of which there must be at least two.

Different classes of shares can be issued:

- ordinary shares (*actions de capital ordinaires*);
- preferred shares (*actions de capital privilegiées*);
- shares without voting rights (*actions sans droit de vote*);
- shares not representing share capital (*parts de fondateur*).

The shares may be bearer shares or issued to a named party. A register of registered shares must be kept at the company containing the following information:

- name and details of the shareholder;
- payments made;
- particulars of any share transfers.

Voting Rights

Each shareholder has a number of votes directly proportional to the number of shares he possesses, without any restriction.

A general meeting of shareholders must be held at least once a year.

The requirements for voting are laid down in the Acte. If nothing is provided in the Acte, resolutions are adopted by simple majority.

Protection of Minority Owners

A general meeting of shareholders must be convened when shareholders representing one-fifth of the capital so request in writing.

There are no restrictions on the number of votes that may be cast by one shareholder. A shareholder has a number of votes in proportion with the number of shares he holds, notwithstanding any restrictions in the Acte.

Transfer of Ownership
The transfer of bearer shares is effected by delivery of the share certificates.

The transfer of registered shares must be recorded in the register of shareholders, which must be signed by both seller and buyer.

Dissolution/Winding Up
The company can be dissolved by the court for special reasons.

Except for dissolution by the court, the company can only be dissolved by decision of the shareholders' meeting taken according to the conditions laid down in the Acte.

Unless stricter conditions are provided in the Acte, if the company has lost half its capital the management must convene a shareholders' meeting within two months of such loss. The shareholders will decide whether or not to dissolve the company by a majority of two-thirds of the shareholders present or represented.

The same applies where the company loses three-quarters of its capital, but here the decision of the shareholders' meeting is adopted with a quarter of the votes of the shareholders present or represented.

Management

Board of Directors
The SA is managed by a board of at least three directors (*administrateurs*). They are appointed for the first time in the Acte. Thereafter they are elected by the shareholders at the general meeting.

The directors are appointed for a maximum of six years but, unless otherwise provided in the Articles of Incorporation, may be re-elected.

The directors need not be shareholders and there is no residence or nationality requirement.

The board has the power to do everything necessary to achieve the object of the company, except for matters that are reserved exclusively to the shareholders, according to the law or to the articles of incorporation.

The Acte determines the number of shares which each director must pledge as guarantee for the performance of his duties. Such shares must be registered shares and the pledge is recorded in the register of shareholders.

The company is bound by the acts of the managing directors even if those acts are not within the objects of the company, unless it can be proven that the third party knew that the act was outside the objects. Knowledge cannot be imputed simply because the Acte was available for public inspection.

Daily Management

The daily management of the company may be delegated to one or more directors or to one or more persons who are not on the board, such as managers, supervisors or other agents. They are appointed in the Acte or by the competent organs of the company.

Employee Representation

Companies with 15 employees or more must have employee delegates (*délégations du personnel*). The delegates must hold at least six meetings a year, including at least three meetings with the management of the company.

Their main task is to communicate with management and to safeguard and defend employee interests regarding working conditions, safety at work and certain benefits.

Employee delegates can only be dismissed in very exceptional circumstances.

A company employing 150 employees or more must have a joint works council (*comité mixte*) composed by an equal number of employers' representatives and employees' representatives.

Statutory Auditors

A large and medium-sized company has to be audited by an independent auditor (*réviseur des entreprises*). A small company is audited by a statutory auditor (*commissaire aux comptes*).

A company qualifies as a small or medium-sized company where it meets two of the following criteria:

- annual turnover of less than LF 160,000,000 for small companies, and of less than LF 640,000,000 for medium-sized companies;
- total balance sheet of less than LF 77,000,000 for small companies and LF 310,000,000 for medium-sized companies;

- has no more than 50 employees for small companies and 250 employees for medium-sized companies.

The auditor is appointed in the articles of incorporation. Where there is more than one auditor they form a 'collège'. They cannot be appointed for a period longer than six years, but can be re-elected by the shareholders.

Formation Expenses and Taxation

Costs of Registering and Forming a Company
The expenditure involved, which is tax deductible, includes the following:

- registration tax of one per cent of the subscribed capital;
- notarial fees, calculated as a proportion of the share capital;
- registration with the 'Registre aux Firmes' (LF 2,400 where the capital is LF 1,000,000 or less, LF 4,800 where the capital is more than LF 1,000,000);
- cost of publication in the Official Gazette, registration of proxies, copies etc (between LF 14,000 and LF 74,000).

Company Taxation

General Information
The corporate income tax rate is fixed at 36 per cent for both resident and non-resident companies. A further surcharge of 2 per cent is payable for unemployment contribution tax.

The corporate income tax applies both to the world-wide income of resident companies and to the Luxembourg source income of non-resident companies.

Apart from the corporate income tax payable to the State, a municipal business tax, fixed at approximately 9.09 per cent of the taxable income, is levied on behalf of the communes; it is deductible for corporate income tax.

The corporate income tax is levied on the corporation. It is also levied on the distribution to the shareholders except where investment of 25 per cent fulfils certain conditions.

The tax year is the calendar year unless otherwise approved by the Inland Revenue.

Taxable Events
Capital gains are taxable as ordinary income. Exempted are gains on sale of buildings or nondepreciable assets such as land that has been

held for more than five years, provided reinvestment of the proceeds are made within two years in other fixed assets for use in the business in Luxembourg. The same exemption applies to gains on the sale of investments held for a minimum of five years. A restriction is imposed in relation to reinvesting the proceeds in shares of another company, in that the Minister of Finance must agree to both the sale and reinvestment in shares.

Tax may be deferred by reinvestment of gains from certain fixed assets if the reinvestment is made in business assets and within the following two years.

Also exempt are dividends from Luxembourg shareholdings of at least 10 per cent if held for twelve months preceding the year in which the dividends were received.

Losses cannot be carried back but may be carried forward for five years by residents and also by non-residents if so provided by tax treaties.

A straight-line method of depreciation is applied in the case of buildings (1.5 to 5 per cent), office equipment (10 per cent) and machinery (20 per cent).

A declining balance method for up to 20 per cent is available except for intangible assets and buildings.

Tax Incentives

For the first eight years of corporation, 25 per cent of the taxable income may be exempted from tax.

Investment credits are available and may be deducted from corporate income tax. These are restricted to new tangible assets not including buildings and motor vehicles.

Further supplementary investments may be deducted by 12 per cent from corporate income tax, provided the assets have a minimum life of four years.

Investment credit tax can be carried forward for four years.

Fundamental Legislative Texts

- *Loi du 10 Août 1915 concernant les sociétés commerciales* (as subsequently amended);
- *Loi du 23 Décembre 1909 portant création d'un registre de commerce et des sociétés* (as subsequently amended);
- Commercial Code Arts 8 to 17 and Art 189;
- *Loi du 28 Juin 1984 portant organisation de la profession de réviseur d'entreprises*;

- *Loi du 6 Mai 1974 instituant des comités mixtes dans les entreprises du secteur privé*, amended by *Loi du 18 Mai 1979;*
- *Loi du 18 Mai 1979 portant réforme des délégations du personnel,* amended by *Loi du 3 Avril 1980.*

THE
NETHERLANDS

PRIVATE COMPANY
(Besloten Vennootschap)

PUBLIC COMPANY
(Naamloze Vennootschap)

INTRODUCTION

This section deals with two types of limited liability company. The first is the Dutch *Besloten Vennootschap* (BV), referred to as a private company. The second is the Dutch *Naamloze Vennootschap* (NV), referred to as a public company.

The legal and administrative requirements to incorporate and administer a BV or an NV are very similar. The major differences between them are in the size of the share capital and the nature of the shares.

The minimum legal capital for the BV is Dfl 40,000 and for the NV Dfl 100,000. The BV can only have registered shares and is not allowed to issue share certificates, whereas the NV can issue registered or bearer shares and may issue share certificates. The articles of association of the BV must contain certain restrictions on share transfers, while the articles of association of the NV need not contain such restrictions.

Both the BV and the SA must have a two-tier board management with a supervisory board where they meet the following criteria:

- the issued capital together with the reserves amounts to at least Dfl 22,500,000;
- the company is required to to have a works council;
- the company employs 100 or more employees in the Netherlands.

There are no restrictions under Dutch company law on the nationality of the founders or of the shareholders.

Before a company can be incorporated, approval from the Ministry of Justice must be obtained (*Verklaring van geen Bezwaar*). This may take up to eight weeks.

Exchange control regulations are very liberal and are primarily designed to provide the Central Bank with sufficient information to keep a record of the balance of payments.

A number of transactions that may have a significant impact on the Dutch Guilder are subject to authorisation from The Netherlands Central Bank. Most transactions must anyway be reported to The Netherlands Central Bank regardless whether they are or not subject to authorisation.

Payments between residents and non-residents of more than Dfl 5,000 must be effected through authorised banks and intermediaries and be reported on standard forms.

PRIVATE COMPANY

(Besloten Vennootschap)

Documents

Memorandum and Articles of Association
The statutes which correspond to the memorandum and articles of association must be prepared in Dutch in a notarial document and must include the following information:

- type and official name of the company;
- address of the registered offices;
- objects of the company;
- amount of authorised share capital;
- the amount which is paid up by the incorporator(s) on the shares subscribed for prior to or at the time of formation and the way in which this amount is paid up;
- number and nominal value of shares;
- names and powers of the managing directors;
- provisions with regard to general meetings of shareholders;
- beginning and end of the business year;
- duration of the company if it is not unlimited;
- names of the supervisory board members if such a board is required.

The draft of the statutes must be submitted to the Ministry of Justice for approval (*verklaring van geen bezwaar*) which may take between six and eight weeks.

Any provision in the statutes can be amended, but all such amendments are subject to approval by the Ministry of Justice.

Minute Book
Minute books of director's meetings and shareholders' meetings must be kept.

Accounting Books
The BV must keep books of accounts and records reflecting the rights and obligations of the company at all times.

The extent of information required to be included in the annual accounts depends on the size of the company. Companies are

181

categorised for these purposes as small, medium or large on criteria of value of assets, turnover and number of employees.

The annual accounts consist of the director's report, balance sheet, the profit and loss account and the notes to the accountants.

They must contain such information as will enable a responsible opinion to be formed on the financial position of the company.

Registration Requirements

Chamber of Commerce

A new company must be registered in the Trade Register (*handelsregister*) of the Chamber of Commerce of the district where it has its registered address.

An annual fee is payable for registration with the Chamber.

The following information must be filed with the Trade Register:

- the complete text of the articles of incorporation;
- name of the company;
- description of the business;
- official address;
- the amount of the authorised, issued and paid-up capital;
- name and address of the shareholders where the shares are not fully paid up;
- restrictions on the power to represent the company for each member of the management board;
- name, nationality, address, occupation and signatures of all members of the management board and the supervisory board;
- any suspension of the members of these boards.

The registration number from the Trade Register must appear on all letters and other documents issued by the company.

A new company must also register with the local tax authorities and the social security offices.

Bank Account

A commercial company must open an account with a financial institution in The Netherlands.

Unless proof is given to the notary that money equivalent to the initial share capital has been deposited, the company cannot be incorporated.

A bank statement to this effect must be attached to the original statutes.

VAT Office
A new company must register with the local VAT and social security offices.

Capital Requirements

Minimum Amounts
The minimum authorised, issued and paid up capital is Dfl 40,000 for a BV formed after 1 January 1985.

If the capital exceeds the minimum, at least 20 per cent of the authorised capital must be issued and at least 25 per cent of the issued capital must be paid up.

At the date of incorporation at least 25 per cent of the par value per share issued has to be paid up and the total par value paid up must at least be equal to Dfl 40,000.

Type of Capital Paid In
Subscriptions can be made in cash or in kind.

In the case of contributions in kind it is necessary to describe the assets contributed. The description must include the value of the assets and the valuation methods used. A statement of a registered accountant confirming the value of the assets must be attached to the deed of incorporation.

Limits to Liability
Each shareholder's liability is limited to his contribution to the capital.

Ownership

Type of Ownership
There must be at least two shareholders, although after the formation of the company they may be reduced to one. There is no maximum on the number of shareholders.

The shareholders may be individuals or legal entities, resident or non-resident, and of Dutch or foreign nationality.

The capital is divided into shares with a fixed par value, but a BV may only issue registered shares and the shares cannot be quoted on the stock exchange.

A register with details of the shareholders must be kept at registered offfices of the company. Shareholders have the right to inspèct this register but it is not open for public inspection except where shares are concerned which are not fully paid up.

The following information must be stated in the register of shareholders:

- name and address of the shareholders;
- par value of the shares;
- the amount paid up;
- the transfer of the shares;
- where shares are not fully paid up, the date of the transfer deed must be mentioned.

Voting Rights and Meetings

Unless otherwise provided in the articles of incorporation, all shareholders have a number of votes directly proportional to the number of shares they possess.

The company may issue preferred shares, the holders of which may have certain privileges not enjoyed by ordinary shareholders, including the right to participate in decisions to issue new shares, to veto amendments to the statutes and to appropriate profits to reserves.

A general meeting of the shareholders should take place at least one a year, within six months following the end of the financial year. The general shareholders' meeting retains all powers not delegated to the other corporate bodies. Additional meetings may be called as prescribed by the articles of incorporation.

The usual voting procedure is the simple majority vote, but the articles may require a higher percentage for important matters.

Voting agreements are valid and enforceable.

Protection of Minority Owners

Shareholders who represent at least one-tenth of the share capital have the right to ask the managing board to convene a shareholders' meeting.

Within certain limits, the articles of incorporation can limit the number of votes one shareholder can cast, provided that shareholders with an equal value of shares have the same voting rights.

Transfer of Ownership

Conditions for transfer of shares to third parties are prescribed by law.

The articles of incorporation may provide further restrictions on the share transfers. Such restrictions may require that:

- a shareholder who wishes to transfer his shares first offer them to the other shareholders; or
- prior approval of the company's management bodies be obtained.

Dissolution/Winding Up

The grounds for dissolution are:

- expiration of the term of the company as provided in the articles of incorporation;
- insolvency of the company;
- resolution of the shareholders' meeting;
- by court order in cases defined in the law.

Dissolution of the company must be published in the Official Gazette and in the Trade Register of the Chamber of Commerce.

The company remains in existence as long as required for the winding-up procedure.

Management

Board of Directors

The daily business affairs of the BV are managed by one or more managing directors (*bestuurders*), who may be either natural or legal persons and need not be shareholders or Dutch citizens.

The managing directors are first appointed in the statutes and are subsequently elected by the shareholders' meeting.

The managing board represents the company *vis-à-vis* third parties and is in charge of the daily management of the company.

Limitations on the daily management powers of one or more members of the managing board have an internal effect only and cannot be invoked against third parties.

Supervisory Board

The articles of incorporation can provide for a supervisory board (*Raad van Commissarissen*).

Members of the supervisory board are appointed in the statutes or by the shareholders' meeting. The supervisory directors must be natural persons and their age limit is 72 years.

The supervisory board has supervising and advising but not executive functions.

The managing board must provide the supervisory board with all information necessary for the proper performance of its duties.

The articles of incorporation can provide that the managing board needs prior approval from the supervisory board for certain decisions, but the managing board is not otherwise hierarchically subordinated to the supervisory board.

A 'large' BV must have a two-tier management structure with supervisory board and managing board unless it is an 'exempted' large company.

The criteria for a 'large' company are the following:

- share capital and reserves amount to Dfl 22,500,000 or more
- the company has established a works council to comply with the statutory obligations
- the company employs at least 100 persons in The Netherlands.

Employee Representation

A company with 35 employees or more must establish a works council (*ondernemingsraad*).

The members of the works council are elected by the employees of the company and must themselves be employees who have been with the company at least one year. They are protected against the termination of their employment contract by management.

For certain decisions (eg working hours, safety and health protection) approval of the works council is required. In other matters, including important company decisions, they have only advisory rights. The works council also has the right to receive information on the company's financial situation.

In a large BV, the works council is entitled to recommend candidates for the supervisory board, as well as to object to the appointment of other proposed candidates.

Statutory Auditors

The BV need not appoint a statutory auditor unless the company meets any of the following criteria:

- the share capital is Dfl 500,000 or more;
- the total balance sheet exceeds Dfl 8,000,000 and the company employs more than 100 employees in The Netherlands;
- the company operates in the insurance or banking sector.

The statutory auditor is either a member of the Institute of Registered Accountants, or an auditor with foreign qualifications who has obtained a licence from the Ministry of Economic Affairs.

The auditors are appointed at the general shareholders' meeting. If the shareholders do not appoint an auditor, the supervisory board or the managing board are authorised to do so.

The statutory auditor must audit the financial situation of the company, the annual accounts and the propriety of the transactions underlying the annual accounts.

The auditor must submit his report to the supervisory board and managing board, and his report has to be attached to the annual accounts.

Formation Expenses and Taxation

Costs of Registering and Forming a Company
The expenditure involved, which is tax deductible, includes the following:

- capital tax of one per cent on the subscribed capital;
- notarial fees between Dfl 1,000 and Dfl 9,000 depending on the size of the share capital;
- registration with the Chamber of Commerce;
- publication in the Official Gazette.

Corporate Income Tax
The corporate tax rate is 42 per cent.

The current Corporation Income Tax Act distinguishes between resident and non-resident companies.

Non-resident companies are subject to Dutch corporate income tax only on income from certain sources:

- business of a permanent establishment in The Netherlands;
- real estate in The Netherlands;
- loans secured by mortgage on Dutch real estate;
- share in the net profits of a business in The Netherlands.

Companies resident in The Netherlands (incorporated in accordance with Dutch company law or companies with their central management in The Netherlands) are taxed on their world-wide taxable income.

Dividend income is free of Dutch corporation tax if the Dutch company qualifies for the participation exemption.

All other income, including capital gains, is deemed to be business income.

Losses can be carried back for three years and carried forward for eight years. Losses incurred in the first six years of the company's operation can be carried forward for an indefinite period of time.

For companies resident in The Netherlands double taxation may be avoided by treaties. In the absence of a double tax treaty Dutch unilateral rules for the avoidance of double taxation may apply.

Fundamental Legislative Texts

The BV is mainly governed by the provisions in Book II, Titel 4 of the Dutch Civil Code, Arts 175 to 284.

PUBLIC COMPANY

(Naamloze Vennootschap)

Documents

Memorandum and Articles of Association

The statutes must be drawn up in the Dutch language in a notarial document and include the following information:

- type and official name of the corporation;
- address of the registered offices;
- objects of the corporation;
- amount of authorised share capital;
- the amount which is paid up by the incorporator(s) on the shares subscribed for prior to or at the time of formation and the way in which this amount is paid up;
- number and nominal value of shares;
- names and powers of the managing directors;
- provisions with regard to general meetings of shareholders;
- beginning and end of the business year;
- duration of the company if it is not unlimited;
- names of the supervisory board members if such a board is required.

The draft of the statutes must be submitted to the Ministry of Justice for approval (*verklaring van geen bezwaar*), which may take between six and eight weeks.

Any provision in the articles of incorporation can be amended, but all such amendments are subject to approval from the Ministry of Justice.

Minute Book

Minute books of directors' meetings and shareholders' meetings must be kept.

Accounting Books

The NV must keep books of accounts and records reflecting the rights and obligations of the company at all times.

The extent of information required to be included in the annual accounts depends on the size of the company. Companies are categorised for these purposes as small, medium or large, on criteria of value of assets, turnover and number of employees.

The annual accounts consist of the director's report, balance sheet, the profit and loss account and the notes to the accountants.

They must contain such information as will enable a responsible opinion to be formed on the financial position of the company.

Registration Requirements

Chamber of Commerce

A new company must be registered in the Trade Register (*handelsregister*) of the Chamber of Commerce of the district where it has its registered address.

An annual fee is payable for registration with the Chamber.

The following information must be filed with the Trade Register:

- the complete text of the articles of incorporation;
- name of the company;
- description of the business;
- official address;
- the amount of the authorised, issued and paid-up capital;
- name and address of the shareholders where the shares are not fully paid up;
- restrictions on the power to represent the company for each member of the management board;
- name, nationality, address, occupation and signatures of all members of the management board and the supervisory board;
- any suspension of the members of these boards.

The registration number from the Trade Register must appear on all letters and other documents issued by the company.

A new company must also register with the local tax authorities and the social security offices.

Bank Account

A commercial company must open an account with a financial institution in The Netherlands.

Unless proof is given to the notary that the money equivalent to the initial share capital has been deposited, the company cannot be incorporated.

A bank statement for this purpose has to be attached to the original statutes.

VAT Office
A new company must register with the local VAT and social security offices.

Capital Requirements

Minimum Amounts
The minimum authorised, issued and paid up capital is Dfl 100,000 for an NV.

Where the capital exceeds the minimum amount, 20 per cent of the authorised capital must be issued and 25 per cent of the issued capital must be paid up.

Type of Capital Paid In
Subscriptions can be made in cash or in kind.

In the case of contributions in kind, it is necessary to describe the assets contributed. The description must include the value of the assets and the valuation methods used. A statement of a registered accountant confirming the value of the assets must be attached to the deed of incorporation.

Limits to Liability
Each shareholder's liability is limited to his contribution to the capital.

Ownership

Type of Ownership
There must be at least two founders for an NV.

The shareholders may be individuals or companies, residents or non-residents.

The capital is divided into shares with a certain par value. Shares with a different par value may be issued but the number of each class of shares must be stated in the articles of incorporation.

The shares may be in the form of bearer shares or registered in the name of a particular party.

A register with names and addresses of holders of registered shares is kept at the registered offices of the company. Any shareholder can obtain a copy of this list of shareholders and a member of the public can obtain a copy with details of partially paid shares.

New shares can only be issued after a decision of the shareholders' meeting. The articles of incorporation can provide that the shareholders' meeting may transfer this power to another organ of the company.

Voting Rights

All shareholders have at least one vote. Voting rights are in proportion to the value of the capital represented by the shares.

The general shareholders' meeting is the supreme authority of the company and is competent for all matters which have not been transferred to the other organs.

The ordinary general meeting is convened at least once a year within six months of the end of the fiscal year.

Resolutions are adopted by a simple majority of the votes present or represented at the meeting. The law and the articles of incorporation can provide for special quorums and majorities for certain matters.

Protection of Minority Owners

Shareholders who represent at least 10 per cent of the share capital have the right to ask the managing board and the supervisory board to convene a general meeting.

Within certain limits, the articles of incorporation can limit the number of votes one shareholder can cast, provided that shareholders with an equal value of shares have the same voting rights.

Transfer of Ownership

The transfer of bearer shares is effected by the mere handing over of the share certificates. Registered shares are transferred by a deed of transfer.

The articles of incorporation can provide for restrictions on the transfer of registered shares. Such restrictions may require that:

- a shareholder who wants to transfer his shares must first offer them to the other shareholders;
- prior approval of one of the company's management bodies be obtained.

Dissolution/Winding Up

The grounds for dissolution are:

- expiration of the term of the company as provided in the articles of incorporation;

- insolvency of the company;
- resolution of the shareholders' meeting;
- court order in cases defined in the law.

Dissolution of the company must be published in the Official Gazette and in the Trade Register of the Chamber of Commerce.

The company remains in existence as long as required for the winding up procedure.

Management

Board of Directors
The NV is managed by one or more managing directors (*bestuurders*), who form the managing board. They may either be natural or legal persons and need not be shareholders or Dutch citizens.

The managing directors are first appointed in the articles of incorporation and are subsequently elected by the shareholders' meeting.

The managing board represents the company *vis-à-vis* third parties and is in charge of the daily management of the company.

Limitations on the daily management powers of one or more members of the managing board have an internal effect only and cannot be invoked against third parties.

Supervisory Board
The articles of incorporation can provide for a supervisory board (*Raad van Commissarissen*).

Members of the supervisory board are appointed in the articles of incorporation or by the shareholders' meeting. The supervisory directors must be natural persons and their age limit is 72 years.

The supervisory board has supervising and advising but no executive functions.

The managing board must provide the supervisory board with all information necessary for the proper performance of its duties.

The articles of incorporation can provide that the managing board needs prior approval from the supervisory board for certain decisions, but the managing board is not otherwise hierarchically subordinated to the supervisory board.

A 'large' NV must have a two-tier management structure, with a supervisory board and managing board, unless it is an 'exempted' large company.

The criteria for a large company are the following:

- share capital and reserves amount to Dfl 22,500,000 or more;
- the company has established a works council to comply with the statutory obligations;
- the company employs at least 100 persons in The Netherlands.

Employee Representation

A company with 35 employees or more must establish a works council (*ondernemingsraad*).

The members of the works council are elected by the employees of the company and must themselves be employees who have been with the company at least one year. They are protected against the termination of their employment contract by management.

For certain decisions (eg working hours, safety and health protection) approval is required. In other matters, including important company decisions, the works council has only advisory rights.

The works council has the right to receive information on the company's financial situation.

In a large NV, the works council is entitled to recommend candidates for the supervisory board, as well as to object to the appointment of other proposed candidates.

Statutory Auditors

A medium sized and large NV must be audited by a statutory auditor where two out of the three following criteria are met:

- annual turnover of Dfl 35,000,000;
- balance sheet totals Dfl 17,000,000;
- annual average of 249 persons employed.

The auditor must be either a member of the Institute of Registered Accountants, or an auditor with a foreign qualification who has obtained a licence from the Ministry of Economic Affairs.

Auditors are appointed at the general shareholders' meeting. If the shareholders do not appoint an auditor, the supervisory board or the management board are authorised to do so.

The statutory auditor must audit the financial situation of the company, the annual accounts and the propriety of the transactions underlying the annual accounts.

The auditor must submit his report to the supervisory board and managing board, and his report has to be attached to the annual accounts.

Formation Expenses and Taxation

Costs of Registering and Forming a Company

The expenditure involved, which is tax deductible, includes the following:

- registration tax of one per cent of the subscribed capital;
- notarial fees between Dfl 1,000 and Dfl 9,000 depending on the size of the share capital;
- registration with the Chamber of Commerce;
- publication in the Official Gazette.

Corporate Income Tax

The corporate tax rate is 42 per cent.

The Corporation Income Tax Act distinguishes between resident and non-resident companies.

Non-resident companies are subject to Dutch corporate income tax only on income from certain sources:

- business of a permanent establishment in The Netherlands;
- real estate in The Netherlands;
- loans secured by mortgage on Dutch real estate;
- share in the net profits of a business in The Netherlands.

Companies resident in The Netherlands (incorporated in accordance with Dutch company law or companies with their central management in The Netherlands) are taxed on their world-wide taxable income.

Dividend income is free of Dutch corporation tax if the Dutch company qualifies for the participation exemption.

All other income, including capital gains, is deemed to be business income.

Losses can be carried back for three years and carried forward for eight years. Losses incurred in the first six years of the company's operation can be carried forward for an indefinite period of time.

For companies resident in The Netherlands double taxation may be avoided by treaties. In the absence of a double tax treaty Dutch unilateral rules for the avoidance of double taxation may apply.

Fundamental Legislative Texts

The NV is mainly governed by Book II, Titel 3 of the Dutch Civil Code, Articles 64 to 174.

PORTUGAL

PRIVATE COMPANY
(Sociedades por Quotas)

PUBLIC COMPANY
(Sociedade Anonima)

INTRODUCTION

Prior to 1 November 1986, when a new Companies Code (*Codigo das Sociedades Commerciais*) came into effect, legal provisions regulating company formation in Portugal were scattered through various legislative enactments, including the 1888 Commercial Code.

The 1986 Code attempts to harmonise and codify the earlier provisions into a single text, as well as to adapt Portuguese commercial law to various EC directives. Generally the Code provides only minimum standards, leaving the founders and participants in these companies and corporation great freedom to structure and conduct their organisations.

The new legislation provides four principal company forms:

- the Private Limited Liability or Quota Company (*Sociedades por Quotas de Responsabilidade Limitada*, abbreviated to Lda) which has a limited number of participants;
- a Corporation (*Sociedade Anonima de Responsabilidade Limitada*, abbreviated to SA), the shares of which may be held by either a small or a wide range of shareholders;
- the Company with Unlimited Liability, or Partnership (*Sociedade en Nome Colectivo*, abbreviated to SNC);
- two types of limited partnership, the *Sociedade en Commandita Simple*, and the *Sociedade in Commandita por accoes*.

This memorandum outlines briefly the basic characteristics of the Quota Company and the Corporation, which are the most useful vehicles for the international businessman seeking to establish a presence in Portugal before 1992.

The Quota Company form is generally preferred for smaller, closely-held enterprises, where flexibility of administration is important, and capital is not required from the investing public. The administration of a Corporation is more complex, although, by contrast with a Quota Company, capital or share ownership may be more easily transferable. It is a vehicle which may be owned either by a small group of shareholders, or expanded to attract public investment through registration on the stock exchange.

198

Portugal at present has an exchange control system of which foreign investors should be aware. Consequently, capital invested in a Portuguese company of whatever type must be registered with the Foreign Investment Institute (*Instituto do Investmento Estrangeiro*) and an import licence obtained in order to assure its repatriation when wanted, and to take advantage of incentive schemes in special sectors such as tourism. While restrictions eventually will be modified to conform with EC policy, for the moment they are still in full force and effect. All non-EC foreign direct investment must as a matter of course be approved in advance by the Institute.

Portuguese company taxation, as of November 1988, is discussed only briefly due to impending important legislative changes.

PRIVATE COMPANY

(Sociedades por Quotas)

Documents

Memorandum and Articles of Association (Contrato de Sociedade)

To form a Quota Company at least two founders, unless the law requires a greater number, must appear before a notary public and execute the Company's *Contrato de Sociedade* (hereafter Contrato), which is a combination of a memorandum and articles of association or by-laws.

This document must contain as a minimum:

- the name, type, duration and object of the company, the capital, registered office, names of founding members;
- the amount of each quota of capital and the identity of its holder;
- the amount subscribed by each company member at the date of its formation, and the amounts paid in and deferred;
- description and valuation of capital paid in kind.

In addition, the Contrato, subject to the minimum standards of the Commercial Code, normally provides the general internal rules by which a company is conducted, including quorum and voting requirements and procedures for amending the Contrato itself.

Minute and Other Books:

A record of all meetings must be kept, and each minute must be signed by those quotaholders who attended. Standard accounting books and ledgers must also be kept by the company auditor, as well as a Quotaholder Registry.

Registration Requirements

The company does not acquire an independent legal existence until the Contrato has been filed with the National Registry of Legal Entities (*Registro Nacional de Pessoas Colectivas*) and the Commercial Registry of its domicile.

A certificate from the National Registry must also be obtained and filed to the effect that the company's name is not already used by another entity, or is not unduly similar to that used by another entity. The Contrato must be published in the Official Gazette (*Diario da Republica*) and in a newspaper of general circulation in the company's domicile.

This registration procedure takes eight to ten weeks.

Capital Requirements

General Observations
Unlike in an SA, the capital of a Quota Company is not divided into shares represented by certificates of equal par value. Each investor instead receives one quota, reflecting his total contribution which is set forth in the Contrato. The quotas may therefore vary in value.

Minimum Amount
The 1986 Code increased a Quota Company's minimum capital to Esc 400,000. Quota Companies already existing on 1 November 1986 are given three years in which to increase their capital to this level, either by capitalising reserves or by injecting additional capital.

Each quota must have a minimum value of Esc 20,000, and be in amounts divisible by Esc 250.

Type of Capital Paid In
At least half of the capital at the time of formation must be paid in cash, which must be deposited in a bank account in the company's name.

Payments of capital contributions which are subscribed but not made when the company is organised cannot be deferred for more than five years from the date of the Contrato.

If a quotaholder does not pay the amount prescribed within the prescribed time, he may, upon notice by the company, forfeit his quota either totally or in part.

Capital contributions made in kind cannot include labour or services.

The total amount subscribed in cash and the nominal value of any assets contributed must total at least the minimum capital prescribed by law for Quota Companies.

Limits to Liability
Quotaholders are liable to third parties only to the extent of their capital contribution. They are, of course, liable to the company to pay in the amounts they have subscribed.

Ownership

Type of Ownership

The ownership of a quota is evidenced only by an annotation in the Contrato's file at the Company Registry. Consequently there are no bearer or nominative share certificates as in the case of an SA.

Although quotas generally are indivisible, if permitted by the Contrato quotas may have co-owners for amounts divisible by Esc 20,000. The co-owners may appoint a common representative to act for and represent them.

Quotaholders

Quotas may be held by resident or non-resident individuals or entities. A minimum of two quotaholders is required to form the company. There is no maximum number of quotaholders required by law.

Profits are divisible among quotaholders in proportion to their ownership, provided that after distribution the mandatory legal reserve does not fall below Esc 200,000.

Voting Rights and Quotaholder Meetings

Generally the Contrato establishes the rules and procedures for calling and conducting quotaholder meetings. By law, however, quotaholders must meet either in Portugal or abroad before 31 March of each year to approve or modify the managers' annual report and accounts. The company management must call the meeting.

Quotaholders must receive notice of a meeting by registered letter at least 15 days in advance. Notice may be waived by the unanimous written agreement of all the quotaholders, except where amendment of the Contrato or dissolution of the company is to be considered. Notice will also be waived if all quotaholders are present at a meeting and agree to waiver.

A quotaholder may elect to be represented by written proxy at a meeting, but only by a spouse, heir or another quotaholder unless the Contrato provides otherwise. Quotaholders are entitled to cast one vote for every Esc 250 they own of the nominal capital.

The subjects which may be discussed and voted upon at meetings include:

- increases in capital;
- redemption, acquisition, disposal, division or cancellation of quotas;

- expulsion of quotaholders;
- election and dismissal of managers, auditors and members of the supervisory boards;
- approval or rejection of the managers' annual report and the financial accounts;
- merger, transformation and dissolution.

Unless the Contrato or the law provide otherwise, most decisions may be taken by a majority vote of the quotaholders present regardless of the percentage of the capital they represent. Resolutions to amend the Contrato, to increase or decrease capital or to dissolve the company, however, must receive the affirmative vote of the owners of 75 per cent of the capital of the company unless the Contrato requires a higher majority. Quotaholders have preferential rights to subscribe to capital increases in money.

Protection of Minority Owners
The managers of a Quota Company must call a quotaholders' meeting if requested by at least 10 per cent of the quotaholders. The request must indicate the matters to be discussed. If the managers refuse, the requesting quotaholders may themselves call the meeting.

Certain decisions of quotaholder meetings may be challenged as against the law or contrary to the best interests of the company in court by quotaholders who did not vote in favour of the decision in question.

Transfer of Ownership
The transfer of ownership of a quota only becomes effective when made by a notarial document and registered with the *Registro Comercial*.

The transferor of a quota remains jointly liable with the transferee to the company for the unpaid amount of his subscription at the time the company is notified of the transfer.

The Contrato may place restrictions on quota transferability.

Dissolution/Winding Up
A Quota Company may be dissolved according to the terms of its Contrato and also by:

- the expiry of the company's duration as provided in the Contrato;
- the supervening illegality of the company's purpose;

- the accomplishment of the company's objective;
- the declaration of the company's bankruptcy.

As a matter of procedure a majority of the quotaholders must confirm the dissolution in the first three instances and request a notarial declaration hereof.

A company may also be dissolved by a judicial decision when:

- for over a year the number of quotaholders has been below the number required by law;
- the object of the company has become impossible to realise;
- for five consecutive years the company has not carried on any business;
- the company carries on an activity not included within its contractual objectives.

Otherwise, a decision to dissolve can only be taken by an affirmative vote of quotaholders representing three-quarters of the company's capital, unless the Contrato requires a greater majority or imposes other conditions. A simple agreement by quotaholders to dissolve is not sufficient. A formal resolution at a duly constituted meeting is required.

Management

Board of Management

A Quota Company must be administered and run by at least one manager. The first manager(s) is designated in the Contrato. Subsequent managers are elected by the quotaholders in the manner established in the Contrato.

Managers need not be quotaholders, Portuguese citizens or residents of Portugal. The board of managers may meet in Portugal or abroad. If a manager's term of office is not fixed, he continues in office until he resigns or is dismissed.

Managers are empowered to carry out all acts necessary to attain the company's objectives, and may bind the company through contracts with third parties. They may not, absent consent of the quotaholders, carry on activities or businesses in competition with those carried on by the company.

Financial Supervision

A Quota Company, unlike a Corporation or SA, is not required by law to have a board of auditors (*Conselho Fiscal*). If, however, the

Contrato so provides, the financial affairs of a Quota Company may, like those of a Corporation, be supervised by a board of auditors. In such cases the articles in the Companies Code on auditors of SAs will apply.

Quota Companies which do not have boards of auditors must appoint a statutory auditor to examine the company accounts if during two consecutive years any two of the following limits are exceeded:

- annual net sales and receipts of Esc 280,000,000;
- the balance sheet of Esc 140,000,000; or
- the average number of employees is more than 50 in any one year.

Formation Expenses and Taxation

Stamp Tax
This is calculated at a rate of one per cent on subscribed capital, even if not paid up.

Notarial Fee
A flat fee of Esc 1,000 is due for the Contrato, plus an additional fee of Esc 100 per page.

A sliding scale of supplementary fees based on each Esc 1,000 of capital, or a fraction thereof, must also be paid as follows:

- up to Esc 200,000: 10 Esc;
- Esc 200,000-Esc 1,000,000: 5 Esc;
- Esc 1,000,000-Esc 10,000,000: 4 Esc;
- over Esc 10,000,000: 3 Esc.

An additional 30 per cent surcharge is added where the company is being newly formed.

Registration Fees
For registering a company at the Commercial Registry a fee of Esc 1,000 must be paid. A further fee of Esc 1,500 is payable on registering the Contrato, plus variable charges depending on the capitalisation in accordance with the above scale of notarial fees.

National Registry of Collective Persons Fees
- a fee of Esc 1,000 is charged upon requesting certification of approval for the company name;

- a fee of Esc 3,000 is due upon issuance of the said certificate;
- a fee of Esc 1,000 is charged upon registration of the Contrato.

Property Transfer Tax (SISA)

The transfer by a quotaholder of real property to a Quota Company as a capital contribution is taxed at a rate of 8 per cent or 10 per cent depending on the nature of the property transferred.

Company Taxation

A company must pay the following annual taxes on profits:

- industrial tax: 30 per cent up to Esc 3,000,000 and 35 per cent thereafter;
- municipal surcharge: 8 per cent to 10 per cent, depending on the municipality;
- special profits tax: 2.5 per cent;
- undistributed profits or complementary tax:
  up to Esc 150,000 – 6 per cent, Esc 150,000 – 1,500,000 — 8 per cent, Esc 1,500,000-7,500,000 — 10 per cent, Esc 7,500,000 — 12 per cent.

Fundamental Legislative Texts

- *Codigo das Sociedades Comerciais, Decreto Lei 262/86* of 2 September 1986;
- *Codigo do Registro Comercial, Decreto Lei 403/86* of 3 September 1986.

PUBLIC COMPANY

(Sociedade Anonima)

Documents

Memorandum and Articles of Association
To form an SA at least five founders must execute a deed before a Notary Public which will constitute the company's 'Contrato', and which, as in the case of a Quota Company, is a combination of the memorandum and articles of association or by-laws. There are no nationality or residence requirements for shareholders.

The Contrato must contain as a minimum the following information:

- the name, domicile, purpose and duration of the company;
- the amount and type of capital paid in, and the time fixed for paying in the remainder;
- the nominal value and number of shares, whether they are nominative or bearer, and the rules for their eventual conversion from one form to the other;
- any special conditions governing share transfers;
- the types of shares which may be created, with an express indication of the number of shares in each category and the rights attaching thereto;
- the authority, if applicable, for issuing bonds and debentures;
- the rules and structure for the administration and financial supervision of the company.

Share Register and Other Records and Books
The share register must be kept at the principal office of the company and contain a description of the shares issued, and, if nominative, indicate their owners. It must be open for inspection by the shareholders.

Accounting books and ledgers must also be kept by the auditors, in addition to a book in which the minutes of shareholder meetings are kept and signed by all those present at each meeting.

Registration Requirements

As with a Quota Company, an SA only acquires legal personality after the Contrato has been registered with the National Registry of Legal Entities and with the *Registro Comercial* in the Corporation's domicile.

As with Quota Companies, a certificate must be obtained from the National Registry of Legal Entities approving the corporate name.

The Contrato must also be registered with the Tax Division of the Ministry of Finance and be published in both the Official Gazette and a daily newspaper of general circulation in the Corporation's domicile. If subscriptions will be solicited from the general public, publication of the Contrato must also be made in a Lisbon or Oporto newspaper.

The registration procedure takes eight to ten weeks.

Capital Requirements

Minimum Amounts

The minimum capital is Esc 5,000,000, represented by shares with a par value of not less than Esc 1,000. Each share is indivisible. Companies established prior to 1986 and with capital below the new minimum have three years in which to increase capital either by capitalising reserves or injecting new amounts.

Type of Capital Paid In

A minimum of 30 per cent of the share capital must be paid up in cash, with the balance due within five years. This amount must be deposited prior to the signature of the Contrato in a bank account in the name of the proposed company. It can only be drawn upon when the company is registered.

Shares cannot be issued for services, although subscriptions in kind can be made.

Capital cannot be increased until the full amount of the original capital is paid in.

Limits to Liability

Shareholders are only liable to the extent of their capital contributions.

If, however, as in a Quota Company, the number of shareholders is reduced to one, he may become completely liable without limitation for the company's obligations.

Ownership

Privately Held or Close Corporations
A minimum of five shareholders is required for a privately held company.

Publicly Held Corporations
These are distinguished from privately held corporations, and special requirements for their formation and public offering are set forth in Arts 279 to 284 of the Companies Code. Basically, the same capitalisation and administration requirements for privately held companies also apply, although if a corporation is formed with the intention of going public, only one promoter need sign the notarial deed constituting the Contrato.

Types of Shares
Shares may be nominative or bearer. If nominative, their ownership must be recorded in the share register and they must be deposited with a commercial bank in the name of the shareholder.

Normally shares can be converted at the holder's request from bearer to nominative, and, unless forbidden by law, vice-versa.

Shares must remain nominative, however, as long as they are not fully paid in, or when the Contrato prohibits their transfer without the consent of the company, or when their transferability is otherwise restricted.

Non-voting preferred shares of the capital may be issued if not prohibited by the Contrato. Holders of non-voting preferred stock may have a right to a fixed dividend of not less than 5 per cent of the nominal value of their holdings, as well as to all the other rights of ordinary shareholders except the right to vote.

Subject to the Contrato, a Corporation may issue bonds as well as equity.

Voting Rights and Shareholders' Meetings
Every share is entitled to one vote, although the Contrato may provide for non-voting preferential shares. Shareholders can vote by written proxy.

Types of Meetings
Unlike legislation in other countries, the new Code does not specifically distinguish between types of meetings of voting share-holders. All their meetings are simply called ordinary meetings. The

210

meetings of preferred shareholders are, however, called special meetings.

In practice, a distinction can be made, however, between the annual general meeting required by law, and ordinary shareholder meetings convened throughout the year for specific purposes.

At least one meeting of the ordinary voting shareholders must be called by the President, the board of directors, or the statutory board of auditors and held within the first three months of each calendar year. It approves the company accounts and directors' reports for the preceding year, elects directors, and decides upon the distribution and use of any profits. The meeting also elects the President and other officers for terms not exceeding four years.

Notice Requirements
Notice of any meeting must be published in the Official Gazette and in a newspaper of general circulation. At least one month must elapse between the date of last publication and the date of the meeting. When all the shares are nominative, notice by registered letter may be given at least 21 days before the meeting.

The notice must state the day, time, place and purpose of the meeting, and whether it is general or special. As in a Quota Company, no notice is required if all shareholders are present and waive notice. Similarly, if shareholders agree unanimously in writing their decisions will be valid and binding even without a formal meeting.

Quorum and Voting Requirements
Unless a specific quorum is required by the Contrato, a meeting will be validly constituted on the first call no matter how many shareholders are present or represented. Resolutions normally can be passed by a majority vote of the shareholders present regardless of the capital they represent.

If, however, the meeting is to decide on amending the Contrato, re-organisation, merger, liquidation or other decisions for which the law requires a particular majority, there must be present or represented a quorum of shareholders holding at least one-third of the capital. Decisions on these important matters may only be approved by the affirmative vote of two-thirds of the issued voting shares, no matter how many shares may be present or represented.

If there is an insufficient quorum for the first meeting, a second call will be made for another meeting to be held in at least 15 days.

On the second call the meeting will be validly held whatever number of shareholders are present or represented. Where at a second call meeting at least half the voting capital is present or represented, resolutions approving amending the Contrato, reorganisation, merger or liquidation require the affirmative vote of a majority of the voting shares present or represented.

Shareholders can be represented by proxy, provided the proxy holder is another shareholder, a member of the board of directors, the spouse or an heir.

Protection of Minority Owners

A meeting also may be called at the request of one or more shareholders representing at least 5 per cent of the voting capital. If the company President refuses the request, shareholders may seek a court order compelling the meeting to be held. The same notice requirements for other meetings will apply.

As in Quota Companies, shareholders of an SA may challenge the validity of decisions made at meetings which have not been properly convened and at which they were not present or represented, or which are in violation of the law or the Contrato.

Further protection is provided by Code provisions not found in prior legislation which give shareholders having at least one per cent of the shares, bondholders, and creditors holding shares as security for loans, the right to demand and receive from the management current information on the Corporation's business and financial status.

Transfer of Ownership

Nominative shares may be transferred by a notarised declaration in writing from the owner to the company officer in charge of the share registry book. First refusal rights may be provided in the Contrato.

Bearer shares are transferred by delivery of the certificates.

Dissolution/Winding Up

The shareholders may agree to dissolve the company at a meeting held on the first call provided that:

- there is a quorum of at least one-third of the capital present or represented; and
- two-thirds of the total issued share capital votes for dissolution.

Shareholders may vote to dissolve the company on the second call provided that:

- at least half the capital is present and represented; and
- a majority of the total issued share capital votes for dissolution.

The Contrato may, of course, impose higher quorum and voting requirements for both calls. Corporations may also be dissolved upon the occurrence of the same events of dissolution as the Code prescribes for Quota Companies, including expiry of the corporate duration, attainment of its objectives, and the subsequent illegality of the corporate objective. In such cases, as with Quota Companies, the shareholders by a simple majority will recognise the dissolution, and then any one of them or a creditor may request a notarial acknowledgement thereof.

A judicial dissolution may also be requested if after one year the number of shareholders falls below that required by law.

Management

The Code provides corporations with two optional forms of administration and management.

One option is the traditional or two-tier form, the components of which are a board of directors (*Conselho de Administraçao*) and a board of auditors (*Conselho Fiscal*).

The other, a new, three-tier form, is composed of the directorate (*Direcçao*), the general board (*Conselho Geral*) and a statutory auditor (*Revisor Oficial de Contas*).

The Contrato must state by which of the two systems the corporation will be managed.

Traditional or Two-Tier Form

Board of Directors (Conselho de Administraçao)
Members of the board of directors are appointed initially in the Contrato, and elected thereafter by the shareholders at their annual meetings according to procedures established in the Contrato for terms not exceeding four years.

The number of directors, who cannot be shareholders, is fixed by the Contrato and must always be uneven. Corporations with a capital not exceeding Esc 20,000,000 need only have one director.

The Contrato may provide that a minority holding at least 10 per cent of the voting capital may elect and be represented by its own director.

The board of directors is charged with the general management of the corporation's activities, and represents the corporation either

213

collectively, or by the specific designation of one or more of its members, in dealings with third parties.

A simple majority is sufficient for a quorum at directors' meetings, and decisions are made by the majority vote of those present or represented. The directors need not be Portuguese citizens, and meetings may be held in Portugal or abroad.

The directors' actions in the name of the corporation bind it in its dealings with third parties, unless it can be shown that the third parties were aware that the directors were acting outside their authority and without shareholder approval.

Directors are under an obligation to conduct the affairs of the company with due diligence. They are liable in damages to the company, shareholders and creditors for violation of the Contrato and the law.

The Board of Auditors (Conselho Fiscal)

This board acts as a check upon the board of directors and is charged with the general supervision of the corporation. It is composed of either three or five members elected by the shareholders for terms not exceeding four years. If the board is of three members, either one or two alternate members must be elected. A five-member board requires at least two alternates. At least one member of the board must be a certified auditor or an auditing firm. Corporations capitalised at less than Esc 20,000,000 need only have one auditor who must, however, be either a certified auditor (Revisor Oficial de Contas) or a qualified firm of statutory auditors.

No member of the board of auditors nor the single auditor may be a shareholder.

The board of auditors must meet at least quarterly. All decisions are taken by majority vote. Records of the meetings and its resolutions must be kept in a special book and signed by the participants. The board's duties include:

- supervision of company activities;
- monitoring compliance with the Contrato and the law in general;
- inspecting and supervising the company accounts and use of funds;
- reporting annually to the shareholders and opining on the board of directors' annual reports;
- convening shareholder meetings when the President fails to call them;

- attending directors' and shareholders' meetings;
- reporting to the Portuguese government any criminal violations it discovers in the performance of its duties.

The board of auditors may also request the President to call a shareholders' meeting if they believe it in the best interests of the company. If he refuses, the board may call the meeting itself, observing the usual notice requirements.

The New Three-Tier Form

The Directorate (Direcçao)

The directorate is composed of an uneven number of no more than five directors, although only one director is necessary where the corporation's capital is less than Esc 20,000,000.

The directors are either appointed in the Contrato or elected by the general council (*Conselho Geral*) for terms not exceeding four years. They can be re-elected. They need not be shareholders, but they cannot be juridical persons or members of the general council. The President of the directorate is appointed by and may be removed by the general council.

The directorate is charged with managing the corporation's activities and with representing the company, subject to the Contrato and instructions from the general council. They are expected to report to the general council at least once a year on management policy, and every quarter before the general council's meeting on the corporation's current financial and business position.

Generally they, or he in the case of a single director, have the same duties and obligations as the *Conselho da Administraçao* in the two-tier management form.

The General Council (Conselho Geral)

The general council is composed of an uneven number of shareholders, which must always be greater than the number of directors but in any case never more than 15. They are either designated in the Contrato or elected at a general shareholders' meeting. The council selects one of its members to act as President.

The council's duties include:

- electing and removing directors;
- representing the company in its relations with the directors;
- reviewing and supervising the actions of the directorate;
- verifying the corporation's financial statements and records;

215

- approving or rejecting the directorate's reports and accounts;
- preparing an annual report for the shareholders;
- calling shareholder meetings as they deem necessary;
- approving or disapproving share transfers.

The Statutory Auditor (Revisor Oficial de Contas)

The statutory auditor, who must not be a shareholder, may be an individual or a firm of certified auditors. He is appointed by the general council for a term of up to three years to examine the company accounts. He has all the duties and powers assigned by the Code to members of the board of auditors (Conselho Fiscal) in the traditional, two-tier type of company administration.

Formation Expenses and Taxation

Stamp Tax

This is calculated at a rate of one per cent on subscribed capital, even if not paid up.

Notarial Fee

A flat fee of Esc 1,000 is due for the Contrato, plus an additional fee of Esc 100 per page.

A sliding scale of supplementary fees based on each Esc 1,000 of capital, or a fraction thereof, must also be paid as follows:

- up to Esc 200,000: 10 Esc;
- Esc 200,000 – 1,000,000: 5 Esc;
- Esc 1,000,000 – 10,000,000: 4 Esc;
- over Esc 10,000,000: 3 Esc.

An additional 30 per cent surcharge is added where the company is being newly incorporated.

Registration Fees

For registering a company at the Commercial Registry a fee of Esc 1,000 must be paid. A further fee of Esc. 1,500 is payable on registering the Contrato, plus variable charges depending on the capitalisation in accordance with the above scale of Notarial Fees.

National Registry of Collective Persons Fees:

- a fee of Esc 1,000 is charged upon requesting certification of approval for the company name;

- a fee of Esc 3,000 is due upon issuance of the said certification;
- a fee of Esc 1,000 is charged upon registration of the Contrato.

Property Transfer Tax (SISA):
The transfer by a shareholder of real property as a capital contribution is taxed at a rate of 8 per cent or 10 per cent depending on the nature of the property transferred.

Company Taxation
A corporation must pay the following annual taxes on profits:

- industrial tax: 30 per cent up to Esc 3,000,000 and 35 per cent thereafter;
- municipal surcharge: 8 per cent to 10 per cent, depending on the municipality;
- special profits tax: 2.5 per cent;
- undistributed or complementary profits tax:
  6 per cent up to Esc 150,000 – 8 per cent between Esc 150,000 and Esc 1,500,000 – 10 per cent between Esc 1,500,000 and Esc 7,500,000 – 12 per cent over Esc 7,500,000.

Fundamental Legislative Texts:

- *Codigo das Sociedades Comerciais, Decreto Lei 262/86* of 2 September 1986;
- *Codigo do Registro Comercial, Decreto Lei 403/86* of 3 September 1986.

SPAIN

PRIVATE COMPANY
(Sociedad de Responsabilidad Limitada)

PUBLIC COMPANY
(Sociedad Anonima)

INTRODUCTION

Under Spanish law the main types of company are the *Sociedad Anonima* (SA) and *Sociedad de Responsabilidad Limitada* (SRL).

The formation requirements of both are very similar. The main differences are:

- in the SA the capital is represented by shares; in the SRL there are participations. Shares are easier to transfer than participations;
- at present there is no minimum or maximum capital for an SA. To form an SRL the maximum capital is Pts 50,000,000; there is no minimum;
- a minimum of 25 per cent of the capital of an SA must be paid up on formation. In the case of an SRL, 100 per cent of the capital must be paid up on formation of the company.

Important modifications in existing legislation will be made by the new law regarding SAs. As of 1 January 1990, the minimum capital for SAs will be Pts 10,000,000, and existing companies will have three years to increase their capital to comply with these requirements or to adopt the form of SRL, which stem from EC legislation. The new Spanish rules are, however, more rigorous than the EC rules, which require a minimum capital of only Pts 4,000,000 in the case of an SA.

The new Law will introduce other important changes, including the requirement to disclose the accounts of the company, and to have these accounts audited by independent accountants.

PRIVATE COMPANY

(Sociedad de Responsabilidad Limitada)

Documents

Memorandum and Articles of Association
To form an SRL all the members of the projected company must agree to and sign before a Notary Public, in person or by proxy, the *Escritura de Constitucion* or memorandum.

The memorandum (which is sometimes called the *Escritura Social*) must contain:

- full name, civil status, nationality and address of the members;
- name;
- object;
- duration;
- registered office and locations where the company will establish branches, agencies and other offices;
- capital and participations into which it is divided;
- goods, shares and cash that each member may contribute to the company;
- appointment of directors of the company;
- form of meetings and procedures for passing resolutions; and
- all other agreements and special conditions to which the members may agree.

Minute Book
General meetings (*Junta General*) are not necessary in all cases. A *Junta General* is not compulsory except where there are 15 or more members or where the memorandum expressly requires it.

If a *Junta General* is not required, resolutions may be made and adopted by post or telegraphic communications or by any other means which may guarantee the authenticity of the decisions taken. Otherwise a minute book should be prepared in the same way as for the SA.

Accounts Books
The administrators of the company must prepare annually the profits and loss account, together with a proposal for profit

distribution. The administrators have five months after the closing of the accounting period to submit the profit and loss account and the balance sheet. There is no requirement to have the accounts audited, but members have the right to examine the accounts in accordance with the memorandum.

Registration Form

Once the memorandum has been prepared and signed before a Notary Public, it must be filed at the Commercial Registry (*Registro Mercantil*). The company has no legal personality until registration.

Registration Requirements

Trade and Industry

Generally, there is only a requirement to register the company at the Commercial Registry. For companies operating in particular fields, registration may be required in other registries established by various ministries.

Tax Authority

Transfer Tax (*Impuesto de Transmisiones*) of 0.75 per cent of the authorised share capital will be paid on formation of the company. The tax authority is the Ministry of Economy and Finance, and payment takes place at the local tax office (*Delegación de Hacienda*). The rate of corporation tax is 35 per cent of net income.

Other Authority

It is necessary to obtain a Code of Fiscal Identity (CIF) number which may be requested at the local tax office.

The company should be registered with the same tax authority for VAT purposes. Prior to registration application for a name must be made to the General Registry of Company Names which is located at the Ministry of Justice (*Registro General de Sociedades*).

Capital Requirements

Minimum Amounts

The SRL requires no minimum capital, although there is a maximum capital of Pts 50,000,000.

Type of Capital Paid In

The capital must be fully paid on formation in cash or in kind.

Limits to Liability

Members are not personally liable for the company's debts except to the extent of their capital contributions.

Ownership

Type of Ownership

The capital will be divided into participations (*participaciones*) which are equal in value, can be accumulated and are indivisible. The number of members cannot exceed 50.

Voting Rights

The *Escritura Social* is the document which establishes the procedure for the meetings and the voting rights of the members. Unless the *Escritura Social* establishes otherwise, resolutions are passed by a majority vote, provided members representing at least 50 per cent of the registered capital are present or represented.

There is no need to call a general meeting if all the members are present and decide to hold a *Junta General* without having called the meeting specifically.

Unless the *Escritura Social* establishes otherwise, every member can be represented by a proxy, who must be an individual but not a legal entity.

Protection of Minority Owners

The administrators of the company must call an extraordinary general meeting if members who represent at least 25 per cent of the capital so request.

The minority can challenge decisions taken in a general meeting if they infringe the law or the *Escritura Social*.

Dissolution/Winding Up

Grounds for dissolution are:

- expiration of the duration term of the company as provided in the memorandum;
- completion of the object of the company or the clear impossibility of achieving it;
- reduction of the capital by more than one-third, unless the capital is restored;
- resolution of the shareholders' meeting by a special majority; and

- judicially declared bankruptcy of the company.

The company remains in existence as long as required for the winding-up procedure. During this time the company must add the words 'in liquidation' to its name.

The liquidators are appointed in the memorandum or by the general meeting of shareholders.

Management

Board
The administrators represent the company. There need only be one administrator.

Where there are several administrators the *Escritura Social* should determine if they can act jointly or independently. If they act jointly the *Escritura* should say whether their decision must be unanimous or by simple majority.

The administrators need not be members, but they must be individuals and not legal entities.

Executive Officers/Management
Executive officers are elected by the board of directors.

Statutory Auditors
No auditors are required for an SRL and members have the right to examine the profit and loss account and the balance sheet, which must be approved by a majority. The period for examination by the members is established by the *Escritura Social*.

Formation Expenses and Taxation

Costs of Registering and Forming a Company
Payment for inscribing the name at the *Registro General de Sociedades* of the Ministry of Justice will cost approximately Pts 500.

Notarial fees for the preparation of the memorandum will vary from notary to notary, but will be in the region of Pts 40-50,000.

Registration at the *Registro Mercantil* will cost approximately Pts 40-50,000.

Taxes on Registered Capital
On formation of a company, a transfer tax at the rate of 0.75 per cent of the share capital must be paid.

Fundamental Legislative Texts

- Law of 17 July 1953 *Ley sobre el Regimen Juridico de las Sociedades de responsabilidad Limitada*;
- where the law is silent or unclear reference should be made to the *Ley de Sociedades Anonimas* of 17 July 1951;
- Code of Commerce of 22 August 1885;
- *Ley de suspension de Pagos* of 26 July 1922;
- *Reglamento del Registro Mercantil* of 14 December 1956.

PUBLIC COMPANY

(Sociedad Anonima)

Documents

Memorandum and Articles of Association

To incorporate an SA, a Notarial Deed called the *Escritura de Constitucion* must be prepared by a Notary Public and must contain as a minimum:

- the identity of the founders of the company, together with nationality and domicile. There must be at least three founders;
- the articles of association (*Estatutos Sociales*) which must include:
  - the name of the company;
  - the object of the company;
  - duration;
  - the date trading is to commence;
  - the company's registered office;
  - the authorised capital;
  - any unpaid capital and procedure to pay it (unpaid capital should not exceed 75 per cent);
  - appointment of administrators; and rules relating to shareholder meetings.

Minute Book

A record of all the meetings should be kept by the secretary of the company. He will prepare the minutes and certified copies of any resolutions, all of which are kept in the minute book (*Libro de Actas*).

Accounts Books

The company should keep annual accounts complying with principles established by the General Accounting Plan (*Plan General de Contabilidad*). The company accounts should include profit and loss statements and balance sheets.

Registration Form

Once the memorandum and articles of association have been signed by the founders before the Notary, the company must be registered in the Commercial Registry (*Registro Mercantil*). The company does not have legal personality until it is registered.

Registration Requirements

Trade and Industry
The company should be registered at the Commercial Registry (*Registro Mercantil*). Generally there is no need to register it with the Ministry of Industry.

Tax Authority
To form a company a person must pay a transfer tax of one per cent on the authorised share capital to the local tax office (*Delegación de Hacienda*), which is a part of the Ministry of Finance. The basic rate of 35 per cent must be paid on the net income.

Other Authority
To obtain a name for the company, application must be made to the General Registry of Company Names (*Registro General de Sociedades*) at the Ministry of Justice.

Capital Requirements

Minimum Amounts
Present legislation does not prescribe a minimum or maximum capital for an SA, although logically it should have sufficient capital to enable it to cover its obligations. Pending legislation will require a minimum capital of Pts 10,000,000 after 1 January, 1990.

Type of Capital Paid In
A minimum 25 per cent of the share capital must be paid up on formation of the company. However, the capital must be fully subscribed.

Limits to Liability
Shareholders are only liable to the extent of their contribution to the company's capital.

Ownership

Type of Shares
There are two main types of shares: bearer shares and registered shares. Bearer shares cannot be transferred unless they have been fully paid.

Voting Rights

A shareholder has voting rights as established by the company's articles. Shares with weighted voting rights are expressly forbidden by law. Shareholders can vote by proxy.

Protection of Minority Owners

An extraordinary general meeting may be called at the request of shareholders representing 10 per cent of paid-up capital.

Shareholders may also challenge resolutions which are contrary to the law or to the memorandum and articles of association, or when they are not in the best interest of the company.

Transfer of Ownership

This is regulated by the company's articles.

The transfer of bearer shares is effected by delivery of the share certificates. The transfer of registered shares is effected via an entry in the Stock Registry.

Dissolution/Winding Up

Grounds for dissolution are:

- expiration of the duration term of the company as provided in the memorandum;
- completion of the object of the company or the clear impossibility of achieving it;
- reduction of the capital by more than one-third, unless the capital is restored;
- resolution of the shareholders' meeting by a special majority; and
- judicially declared bankruptcy of the company.

The company remains in existence as long as required for the winding-up procedure. During this time the company must add the words 'in liquidation' to its name.

The liquidators are appointed in the memorandum and articles of association or by the general meeting of shareholders.

Management

Board

An SA may be governed either by a board of directors or by a sole director. If there is a board of directors, a minimum of three members are required. Directors need not be shareholders, unless otherwise stipulated by the articles. Members of the first board of directors are appointed by the founders of the company. Subsequent boards of directors are appointed according to the procedures established in the articles, and unless otherwise stipulated by them, they are elected for five years.

Executive Officers/Management
Executive officers are elected by the board of directors.

Statutory Auditors
In an SA no auditors are required by law unless the company is listed on the stock exchange or is a bank. Nevertheless, the articles can require the appointment of independent auditors.

Formation Expenses and Taxation

Costs of Registering and Forming a Company
When forming an SA, the following costs will be incurred:

- payment upon requesting name in the General Registry of Company Names (*Registro General de Sociedades*) (approximately Pts 500);
- payment of the notarial fees. This amount varies from notary to notary; between Pts 70,000 and Pts 80,000 is common for an SA with a small capital and small number of shareholders;
- payment of registry fees. The amount is difficult to determine in advance, but it should be between Pts 40,000 and Pts 50,000.

Taxes on Registered Capital
Upon formation of the company a transfer tax (*Impuesto de Transmisiones Patrimoniales*) at a rate of one per cent of the share capital must be paid.

Fundamental Legislative Texts

- *Ley de Sociedades Anonimas* of 17 July 1951;
- Commercial Code of 22 August 1885;
- *Ley de Suspension de Pagos* of 26 July 1922;
- *Reglamento del Registro Mercantil* of 14 December 1956.

UNITED KINGDOM

PRIVATE COMPANY

PUBLIC COMPANY

INTRODUCTION

In the United Kingdom the current incorporation statute is the Companies Act 1985, which provides for various types of registered companies. The two principal types are the private and the public limited company. Due to differences in legal tradition, private and public companies in the UK are not completely equivalent or analogous to private and public companies in continental jurisdictions.

In UK limited liability companies, shareholder liability may be limited either by shares or by guarantee. Unlimited companies and companies limited by guarantee are insignificant in number and importance. The vast majority of companies in existence today are registered private companies limited by shares, although there is a relatively small, but economically powerful, number of public companies limited by shares.

The Companies Act 1985 (hereinafter referred to as the Act) applies to England, Wales and Scotland. In Northern Ireland, the current incorporation statute is the Companies Act (Northern Ireland) 1960 as amended by various Acts and Orders.

The UK government abolished exchange controls in 1979. Furthermore foreign investors are not restricted under UK law from forming or participating in UK companies in any way.

PRIVATE COMPANY

Documents

Memorandum and Articles of Association
A private company is formed by registering certain documents and complying with the procedure specified in the Act.

Every registered company must have a memorandum which regulates the company's external affairs and articles which regulate the company's internal affairs.

The memorandum of a private company must state the following:

- the name of the company, which should end with the word Limited or Ltd;
- the country where the registered office of the company is to be;
- the objects of the company;
- that the liability of members is limited;
- the amount of the share capital of the company;
- that the subscribers to the memorandum wish to form a company;
- the agreement of the subscribers to each take a specified number of shares.

The form of a memorandum must correspond as closely as circumstances permit to that given in Table B of the Companies (Tables A-F) Regulations 1985.

The memorandum must be signed by at least two persons and each must take at least one share (ss 1 (1), 2 of the Act — any further citation of sections without the Act refer to the Act).

The signatures of the two persons who sign must be witnessed by a third person.

The articles of association set out the rules governing the internal management of the company and shall contain:

- the appointment and powers of the directors and secretary;
- the issue and transfer of shares;
- the conduct of meetings;

- voting rights, dividends, accounts, audits.

There are model articles contained in Table A in the Companies (Tables A-F) Regulations 1985. If a company does not register its own set of articles or, if it does, to the extent that they do not modify or exclude Table A, the Table will automatically become the company's articles.

The articles must be signed by the same persons who signed the memorandum (ss 1, 7).

Minute Book

The company must keep books containing the minutes of proceedings at general meetings of the company (ss 382, 383).

Shareholders' Register

Every company must keep a register of its members at its registered office stating the names and addresses and number of shares held by each member and the date at which each person became (and ceased) to be a member. If there are more than 50 members there must be an index (ss 352, 354). The register is to be open for inspection by members and the public during business hours.

Accounting Books

A company must keep accounting books at its registered office or such other place as the directors think fit (ss 221, 222). It is the directors' duty to prepare the annual accounts for the financial year. A copy of the accounts must be filed with the Registrar of Companies no later than six months after the end of the financial year to which they relate.

According to s 228(1) a company's accounts shall comply with the requirements as to the format of balance sheets and profit and loss account of Schedule 4 of the Act.

Section 248 allows for modified accounts for either a small or medium-sized company. A company with less then 50 employees, a balance sheet total of not more than £975,000 and a turnover of not more than £2,000,000 per financial year qualifies as a small company. The equivalent criteria for a medium-sized business are 250 employees, turnover of £8,000,000 and a balance sheet total of £3,900,000.

Registration Form

There are a number of forms for registration purposes which can be obtained from the Registrar of Companies.

The memorandum and the articles of association must be registered with the Registrar of Companies, the files of which are kept at the Companies Registration Office (Cardiff for England and Wales; Edinburgh for Scotland).

Further documents that must be submitted for registration are:

- a statement of the names of the proposed first director or directors, first secretary or joint secretaries and the other particulars specified in Sch 1(companies form No 10);
- a statutory declaration by a solicitor engaged in the formation, or by a person named as director or secretary of the company, of compliance with the requirements of the Act in relation to registration (s 12(3), companies form No 12);
- a statement of formation giving details of authorised capital and of shares taken on registration for assessment of capital duty payable (companies form PUC1);
- Bankers draft or cheque for registration fee and capital duty.

Once the certificate of incorporation has been issued a private company may commence business and exercise borrowing powers.

Company Announcements
Table A of the Companies (Tables A to F) Regulations 1985 provides for notices to shareholders. Notice may be given either personally or by post in a prepaid envelope addressed to the member at his registered address. A member whose registered address is not within the UK and who gives no other address is not entitled to receive any notice. A company's articles may provide otherwise.

Registration Requirements

Trade and Industry
Apart from registration with the Registrar of Companies no further registration is required. Also no permission is required to start a business.

Tax Authority
The relevant tax authority is the Inland Revenue. The company must also register for VAT at the local HM Customs and Excise Office.

Other Authorities
Membership in local Chambers of Commerce is not obligatory.

Capital Requirements

Minimum Amount
No minimum capital requirements for registration or commencement of business exist (ss 11 and 117).

Type of Capital Paid In
Shares allotted by a private company may be paid up in money or kind, including goodwill and know-how (s 99(1)). The valuation provisions contained in the Act (ss 101–116) only apply to public companies. A company's shares may not be allotted at a discount (s 100(1)).

Limits of Liability
Shareholder liability is limited to the sums which they have already contributed to the capital of the company and to any amount still outstanding on their shares up to their par value and any premium on them.

Ownership

Type of Ownership
The articles may divide the issued shares into different classes with different rights as to, for example, voting, dividends, and priority of capital repayment. Commonly a company has ordinary and preference shares. Ordinary shares usually have no guaranteed right to a fixed dividend or priority as to repayment. Preference shares may have the following characteristics:

- they entitle the owner to an annual fixed stated dividend paid in priority to any dividend payments to other shareholders;
- upon winding up, preferential shareholders may be repaid their capital in priority to other shareholders.

Preference shares are regarded as medium-term capital by companies, that is more like debentures although legally they are shares.

A debenture is normally issued as security for a loan and is an instrument executed under the seal of a company, charging the whole or a part of its undertaking or specific property in favour of the holder, to secure the sum loaned and to provide for the payment of interest at a specified rate until the principal has been repaid. Debentures are usually redeemable.

Voting Rights

Ordinary shares usually have full voting rights. Preference shares have limited voting rights.

Protection of Minority Owners

A majority of shares will normally control the company. Although the law supports majority rule it recognises the need to protect the minority in certain circumstances:

At Common Law

Where, for instance, a fraud has been perpetrated on a minority of shareholders by the directors, this minority, as opposed to the company itself, can take legal proceedings unless the majority of shareholders ratify the acts or omissions of the directors at a general meeting.

Under the Companies Act 1985

- s 303 allows for the removal of directors by ordinary resolution;
- There are various rights to object:
  — to variations of class rights (s 127);
  — to an alteration of the company's objects clause (s 5);
- ss 459-61 give the right to apply for a court order on the grounds of unfairly prejudicial conduct, including for example, arbitrary conduct or abuse of controlling power;
- minorities may seek a winding-up order (s 122(1)(g) Insolvency Act 1986);
- minorities may initiate an investigation (s 431 et seq) into the conduct of the company's affairs.

Transfer of Ownership

Sections 183 *et seq* contain detailed provisions on the procedures to be observed for the transfer of shares.

Private companies are forbidden to offer their shares for sale to the public, whether on the stock exchange or otherwise (ss 143 (3), 170, Financial Services Act 1986). Unless the articles provide some form of restriction on transfer, all shares are otherwise freely transferable. Many private companies have restrictive provisions which can take either of two forms:

- pre-emption clause requiring members to offer their shares first to the existing members before they may sell them to outsiders;

- the director(s) may be given the power to refuse to register any transfer of ownership.

Shareholders' Meeting

Every company must hold an annual general meeting in each calendar year. Not more than 15 months shall elapse between one annual meeting and the next. A newly incorporated company must hold its first annual meeting within 18 months of incorporation. The meeting shall be called by 21 days' notice in writing, unless shorter notice has been agreed amongst the shareholders.

Other meetings of shareholders may be called by the company as necessary for specific purposes.

Dissolution/Winding Up

A company may be wound up voluntarily in the following cases (s 84) where:

- the period fixed by the articles for its duration expires or an event occurs which the articles provide is to dissolve the company, and the company passes an ordinary resolution that it be wound up;
- the company passes a special resolution that it be wound up voluntarily;
- the company passes an extraordinary resolution that because of its liabilities it ought to be wound up voluntarily.

According to s 122 Insolvency Act 1986, a company can be wound up by a court order where:

- a special resolution to wind up has been passed by the company;
- business has been suspended by the company for more than one year and there is no intention to carry on a business;
- there are less than two members left;
- the company is unable to pay its debts;
- the court considers that it is just and equitable to do so (eg if there is a justifiable lack of confidence in the management).

Management

Board of Directors

The company operates through agents who are authorised by the shareholders to act on behalf of the company. These agents are the director or board of directors and those to whom the board may have delegated power (Art 70, Table A).

The powers are set out in the articles of association and are fiduciary in nature in that they must be exercised bona fide for the benefit of the company as a whole. These powers include:

- appointing additional and alternate directors;
- binding the company;
- borrowing;
- convening meetings;
- delegating power;
- granting gratuities;
- issuing shares, debentures and negotiable instruments;
- rejecting transfers of shares.

A private company must have at least one director (s 282) but it can appoint more.

Every company must notify the registrar of any changes in respect of its agents and keep a register of its directors and secretary (s 288). This must specify their full names, usual residential address, nationality, business occupation, other directorships and date of birth (s 289).

Company boards may consist of either full-time executive directors or part-time non-executive directors. Executive directors sit on the board but also are employed under a contract to be part of the management of the company.

Non-executive directors are not employees of the company. They generally are part-time and appointed for their knowledge or experience to assist in the policy-making role of the board. They have no individual power as directors to bind the company except collectively as a board, unless the board has appointed any of them to be an agent of the company (Art 71, Table A) or delegated any of its power to any director (Art 72 Table A).

The company must also have a secretary who may not also be the sole director of the company (s 283). The secretary is the chief administrative officer of the company and in administrative matters has ostensible authority to enter contracts on behalf of the company including purchasing office equipment and hiring staff.

The duties of the secretary include:

- taking minutes at meetings;
- making sure that the company's registers are maintained, that its documention is in order and that its returns are correctly made to the registrar;

- notifying members of meetings;
- countersigning documents to which the company seal is attached.

Supervisory Board

UK company law does not provide for representation of employees on a supervisory board. Furthermore, there is no legal requirement for works councils. The employees of a company may be represented by their respective trade unions.

Statutory Auditors

An auditor must be appointed annually by the general meeting (s 384). Only a qualified accountant or a person having requisite experience as such may be appointed (s 389).

The auditor's duty is to examine the company's accounts for a financial year, which the director will lay before a general meeting, and to make a report on those accounts (s 236(1)). It is the duty of the company's auditor to carry out such investigations as will enable him to form an opinion as to whether proper accounting records have been kept by the company and whether the balance sheet is in agreement with the accounting records and returns.

Every auditor of a company has a right of access at all times to the company's books and accounts (s 237).

Formation Expenses and Taxation

Costs of Registering and Forming a Company

According to the Companies (Fees) Regulations 1980, a fee of £50 shall become payable upon registration of a company.

Taxes on Registered Capital and Others

The financial year in the UK is counted from 1 April to 31 March.
The main elements of the UK corporation tax system are:

- resident and non-resident companies that operate in the UK through a branch are liable for corporation tax on profits, whether distributed or not. The current rate for corporation tax is 35 per cent;
- a company is required to make an advance payment to the Inland Revenue of corporation tax (ACT) on distributed

profits. The amount of ACT is calculated by reference to the basic rate of income tax (currently 25 per cent) expressed as a fraction of the cash payment (25/75 of the distributed amount);

- the company can set off any ACT paid against its corporation tax bill for that accounting period;
- the recipient of a distribution in respect of which ACT is payable is entitled to a tax credit;
- special rules as regarding distribution apply to special types of private companies or so called 'close' companies. These are companies which are controlled by five or fewer individuals or directors. Such companies must distribute, subject to a minimum limit, all its investment income and half of its estate income.

Capital gains are taxed at 35 per cent. ACT paid for gains after 17 March 1987 can be set off against the liability. Capital losses can be carried forward against capital gains for an indefinite period.

Trading losses may be set off against any profits of the same or previous period or they may be carried forward indefinitely against income from the same trade.

Depreciation for tax purposes is available for particular types of assets, ie machinery, new industrial buildings, scientific research.

Relief from double taxation is available for a company resident in the UK with income or capital gains from any foreign source. The UK company is entitled to claim credit for foreign taxes paid against the UK tax payable on the same income or gains.

On the formation of a company capital duty of one per cent is due on shares issued (ss 47-49 Finance Act 1973). Duty on the transfer of an existing business to the company of £1 per £100 value becomes payable.

Stamp duty is imposed on documents connected with the transfer of shares and securities, land and certain other assets. The duty is 0.5 per cent for shares and securities and one per cent for other assets.

Local property taxes (rates) are charged on the value of the property. These vary from one local authority to the other. The rates system will be replaced by the poll tax system in the near future.

Fundamental Legislative Texts

- Companies Act 1985;
- Company Security (Insider Dealing) Act 1985;

- Business Names Act 1985;
- Companies Consolidation (Consequential Provisions) Act 1985;
- Insolvency Act 1986;
- Company Directors Disqualification Act 1986;
- Financial Services Act 1986;
- Income and Corporation Taxes Act 1988
- various statutory instruments, rules and regulations, made pursuant to those Acts: eg the Companies Tables (A-F) Regulations 1985 and the Insolvency Rules 1986.

PUBLIC COMPANY

Documents

Memorandum and Articles of Association
All registered companies are presumed to be private unless specially registered as public companies.

Apart from the requirements mentioned above for private companies the memorandum of a public company must contain the following:

- a statement that it is to be a public company (s 1(3)(a));
- an authorised capital figure of £50,000;
- its name must end with the words public limited company or the abbreviation PLC (ss 25(1), 27).

The company must have at least two directors.

Minute Book
The company must keep the general meeting's minute book at its registered office (s 383).

Accounting Book
The same provisions as for private companies apply.

According to s 247, public companies are not entitled to deliver accounts in a modified form as set out by Sch 8.

A copy of the accounts must be filed with the Registrar of Companies no later than ten months after the end of the financial year to which they relate.

Report on Foundation
Instead of a report, a statutory declaration by a solicitor engaged in the formation, or by a person named as director or secretary of the company, of compliance with the requirements of the Acts in relation to registration (s 12(3)) shall be submitted for registration (form no 12).

Company Announcements
The same applies as for private companies.

Shareholders' Register
The same applies as for private companies.

Registration Forms
The memorandum and articles must be registered the same way as for private companies.

Public companies must also acquire a certificate to commence business from the Registrar before they can engage in any trading activity or borrow money (s 117). This is issued when the company has allotted shares to the nominal value of £50,000, paid up to at least one-quarter of that amount (ss 101, 117).

Companies Form No 117 is to be used for application by a public company for a certificate to commence business and a statutory declaration in support.

The Registrar must publish notice of the issue of each certificate of incorporation in the *Gazette*.

Registration Requirements

Trade and Industry
Apart from registration with the Registrar of Companies, no other registration or authorisation is needed.

Tax Authority
The authority is the Inland Revenue. The company must also register for VAT at the local HM Customs and Excise office.

Other Authority
If a company wants to trade its shares at the stock exchange application must be made to the council of the stock exchange for admission of any securities to the official list of the stock exchange.

Membership in a local chamber of commerce is not obligatory.

Capital Requirements

Minimum Amount
The authorised minimum capital is £50,000 (s 11) or such other sum as prescribed by the Secretary of State (s 118). However, a public company need not have called in all that amount. Provided it has allotted shares of £50,000 nominal value its actual contributed

capital may be only one-quarter of the nominal value of each allotted share. The contributed capital therefore may be as little as £12,500 together with the right to call the remaining £37,500 (ss 101(1)(2), 117(4)).

According to s 142, the directors shall call an extraordinary meeting where the net assets of a public company are half or less of its called-up share capital.

Type of Capital Paid In
Public companies cannot accept non-cash consideration for their shares except in the following cases:

- if it is to be transferred to the company within five years and is actually so transferred (s 102);
- if a report on its value has been made by an independent valuer qualified to be the company's auditor at least six months prior to the allotment (s 103).

A public company may not accept as payment for its shares an undertaking given by a person to do work or perform services for the company.

A public company must give itself a lien on its own shares until the full payment of the share has been made. Any provision in the articles to the contrary is void.

Limits to Liability
Shareholder liability is limited to the sums which they have already contributed to the capital of the company, and to any amount still outstanding on their shares up to their par value of those shares and any premium.

Ownership

Type of Ownership
The position as regards share ownership is the same as for private companies.

Voting Rights
Voting rights depend on the type of ownership — ordinary shares have full voting rights, preference shares have limited voting rights.

Protection of Minority Owners
The position is the same for private and public companies.

Transfer of Ownership

If a public company is listed on the stock exchange, restrictions on the transfer of shares cannot be imposed, and the Stock Transfer Act 1963 provides procedures by which shares are transferable.

The strict provisions contained in the Financial Services Act 1986 must be followed regarding advertising to the public via a prospectus.

Shareholders' Meeting

The same rules apply for public companies as for private companies.

However, according to s 142, directors of a public company must call an extraordinary meeting of the company within 28 days of any director knowing that the company has suffered any serious loss of capital (ie that the net assets represent less than half of its paidup capital).

Dissolution/Winding Up

The same applies as for winding up private companies.

In addition, a public company can be wound up by an order of the court if the company has been first registered for more than a year and has no certificate to commence business (s 122(1)(b)).

Management

Board of Directors

In public companies a non-executive director is generally appointed chairman of the board to preside over board meetings, and at general meetings of the company.

The company secretary of a public company must be specially qualified to be appointed to the office. Details are set out in s 286. Otherwise the position is the same as for private companies.

Supervisory Board

UK company law does not provide for representation of employees on a supervisory board. Furthermore, there is no legal requirement for works councils. The employees of a company may be represented by their respective trade unions.

Statutory Auditors

The position as regards auditors is the same for public as it is for private companies.

Formation Expenses and Taxation

Costs of Registering and Forming a Company
According to the Companies (Fees) Regulations 1980, a fee of £50 is payable upon registration of a company on its formation details.

Taxes on Registered Capital
The same applies as for private companies.

Fundamental Legislative Texts

The same legislation applies as for private companies.

USEFUL ADDRESSES

Chambers of Commerce

United Kingdom
London Chamber of Commerce
69 Cannon Street
London EC4N 5AB
Tel: 01-248 4444

Association of Chambers of Commerce
7 Clare Street
Dublin 2
Ireland
Tel: 0001 764291

Other European Community Chambers of Commerce in the United Kingdom
Belgio-Luxembourg Chamber of
Commerce
Sabena House
36-37 Piccadilly
London W1V OPL
Tel: 01-831 3508

The Netherlands-British Chamber of
Commerce
The Dutch House
307-308 High Holborn
London WC1V 7LS
Tel: 01-405 1358

French Chamber of Commerce
2nd Floor, Knightsbridge House
197 Knightsbridge
London SW7 1RB
Tel: 01-225 5250

Portuguese Chamber of Commerce and
Industry
4th Floor, New Bond Street House
1-5 New Bond Street
London W1Y 9PE
Tel: 01-493 9973

German Chamber of Industry and
Commerce
12-13 Suffolk Street
London SW1Y 4HG
Tel: 01-930 7251

Spanish Chamber of Commerce
5 Cavendish Square
London W1M 0DP
Tel: 01-637 9061

Italian Chamber of Commerce
Walmer House
296 Regent Street
London W1R 6AE
Tel: 01-637 3153

Embassies

Belgium
103 Eaton Square
London SW1W 9AB

Italy
14 Three Kings Drive
Davies Street
London W1Y 2EH

Denmark
55 Sloane Square
London SW1X 9SR

Luxembourg
27 Wilton Crescent
London SW1X 8SD

France
58 Knightsbridge
London SW1X 8PZ

Germany (Federal Republic of)
23 Belgrave Square
London SW1X 8PZ

Greece
1a Holland Park
London W11 3TP

Ireland (Republic of)
17 Grosvenor Place
London SW1X 7HR

The Netherlands
38 Hyde Park Gate
London SW7 5DP

Portugal
11 Belgrave Square
London SW1X 8PP

Spain
24 Belgrave Square
London SW1X 8QA

Commission of the European Communities

Commission of the European Communities (UK Office)
8 Storey's Gate
London SW1P 3AT
Tel: 01-222 8122

Commission of the European Communities (Information Unit)
8 Storey's Gate
London SW1P 3AT
Tel: 01-222 8122

Department of Trade and Industry

Department of Trade and Industry (DTI)
1-19 Victoria Street
London SW1H OET
Tel: 01-215 7877

DTI (Exports to Europe Branch)
1 Victoria Street
London SW1H OET

Belgium
01-215 5486

Denmark
01-215 5140

France
Consumer Goods 01-215 4762
Capital Goods 01-215 5197

Federal Republic of Germany
Consumer Goods 01-215 4796
Capital Goods 01-215 5179

Greece
Consumer Goods 01-215 4776
Capital Goods 01-215 5103

Republic of Ireland
01-215 4783

Italy
Consumer Goods 01-215 5103
Capital Goods 01-215 4776

The Netherlands
01-215 4790

Portugal
01-215 4782/5336

Spain
01-215 4782/5336

European Parliament Information Office

2 Queen Anne's Gate
London SW1H 9AA
Tel: 01-222 0411

Brebner & Co

Head Office:
107 Cheapside
London EC2V 6DT
Tel: 01-600 0885

Lloyds Link:
Room 668, 1 Lime Street
London EC3M 7DQ
Tel: 01-929 4730

Dublin Link:
Room 213, Confederation House
Kildare Street
Dublin 2
Tel: 0001 779801

European Desks
France:
1 Bis Avenue Foch
75116 Paris
Tel: 010 33 1 4501 7344

Italy:
Via Olmetto 5
20123 Milano
Tel: 010 39 2 86 06 86

Spain:
Paseo de la Castellana 143
28046 Madrid
Tel: 010 34 1 270 27 81